Immanuel

Immanuel

HANS-RUEDI WEBER

WM. B. EERDMANS, GRAND RAPIDS
WORLD COUNCIL OF CHURCHES, GENEVA

Library of Congress Cataloging in Publication Data
Weber, Hans-Ruedi.
    Immanuel: the coming of Jesus in art and the Bible.
    1. Jesus Christ—Nativity—Meditations.   2. Jesus
Christ—Art.   I. Title.
BT315.2.W36   1984   232.9 ′21   84-8123
ISBN 0–8028–3603–8 (Wm. B. Eerdmans)

Cover design: Paul May, London

Printed and bound in Great Britain at William Clowes Limited,
Beccles and London

ISBN 2–8254–0793–3 (World Council of Churches)

Joint publication 1984 by the World Council of Churches, Geneva,
and Wm. B. Eerdmans Publishing Co., Grand Rapids

Table of contents

Introduction

He shall be called Immanuel,
which means "God with us".

This is the good news with which Christian faith
begins. Each of the four evangelists testified in his own
way how God came among us. Soon, however, these
four testimonies were fused together in the traditional
Christmas story, and legends started to overgrow the
original narratives.

This book is an invitation to rediscover the original
witness to that awesome event of God's coming among
us, of God entering the cruel human world of power
politics as a vulnerable child. Readers should therefore
attempt to set aside for a while the composite picture of
the Christmas crib: kings and angels, shepherds in
sheepskins with a lamb as their gift, the star, an ox and
an ass, camels, Joseph somewhere in the background,
and in the centre Mary with a sweet little baby.

Insights gained from two different approaches will
guide our meditation: first, discoveries made in Bible
studies about the beginnings of the four Gospels;
secondly, visual interpretations of God's coming among
us, provided by artists from many centuries and
cultures. These two main sources of insight will be
complemented by prayers and hymns out of the treasure
of the church's worship throughout the ages.

Not all the works of art reproduced are masterpieces
which will pass the test of time. The choice was made
through a long process of interaction between the
intuitive visual and the analytic reflective interpretation
of a given biblical passage. In this process some
excellent works of art had to be excluded because they
failed to complement the insights gained through the
analysis of texts. On the other hand, some works of
lesser artistic quality are included because the circumstances under which they were created or their special
design and colours do throw a new light on the all too
familiar biblical texts and stories. Moreover, wherever
possible, preference is given to less known artistic
interpretations. Some of the works of art here published
have actually been created on commission for this book.

The prologues to the Gospels of Mark and John, as
well as the birth and infancy narratives in the Good
News according to Matthew and Luke, use highly

evocative, "theopoetic" language. They are full of allusions to the Old Testament and to prevailing expectations in the time of Jesus. Further, they already anticipate the main testimony of each evangelist. The more these biblical passages are seen and understood in their original context, the more they can speak to our own context and life today.

Each of the following units of two pages of text with the accompanying reproduction of an art work can be read on its own and meditated upon. One must then be aware, however, that each unit highlights only one facet of meaning. In order to comprehend the many-splendoured message of the Gospel prologues and childhood narratives it is necessary to let the various units correct and complement one another and to read them within the framework of the whole gospel. This specific frame for the testimony of each evangelist has been sketched in the introduction to the four Gospels.

This book is dedicated to the sisters of the "Communauté de Grandchamp": to their adventure of letting God's incarnation in Jesus Christ penetrate their whole life and ministry as a community of prayer and Christian presence in the world.

May the following biblical reflections and art meditations on the Immanuel lead many to discover the truth of the apostle Paul's affirmation: "We all reflect as in a mirror the splendour of the Lord; thus we are transfigured into his likeness—his icon—from splendour to splendour."

* * *

Modern versions of the four evangelists' symbols appear in Plate 1: the lion and the ox, the figure with a human face, and the eagle.

It is good to recall the origin of these symbols, for they reveal the basic purpose for which the evangelists wrote. They indicate the deepest motivation for believers to examine the Gospel texts, for artists to visually interpret biblical stories, for poets and musicians to enrich the church's liturgy. The origin of these symbols also points to the overall aim of this book.

In a vision John, the writer of the Book of Revelation, was taken up into heaven. There he saw a dazzling sight: the throne of God and around it four living creatures, the first like a lion, the second like an ox, the third with a human face and the fourth like an eagle in flight. He heard them sing the *Sanctus*, without a pause, by day and by night:

Holy, holy, holy is God
the sovereign Lord of all,
who was, and is,
and is to come! (Rev. 4:8)

What John saw and heard must be read in the light of the visions which Isaiah and Ezekiel had when they were called to their prophetic task (Isa. 6; Ezek. 1). The four living creatures had originally been symbols of God's presence, of his power over the entire universe, of the acknowledgment of God's sovereignty by the whole cosmos. From the 3rd century onwards some Christian authors saw these living creatures also as the symbols of the four evangelists: Mark, Luke, Matthew and John. The evangelists too have been in a special way in the presence of the Lord. What they heard and saw, they wrote down as a testimony. And they did so in order that the church might hear and see, and join in the *Sanctus*, the praise of God.

There is thus a deep inner relationship between the four living creatures of the Book of Revelation and the purpose for which the four evangelists wrote. The way in which a particular symbol was assigned to a particular evangelist may be less convincing to modern minds than it was to Jerome, the learned Latin church father, who wrote: "The first figure, that of the human being, represents Matthew because he began his Gospel by speaking about humanity, starting with the genealogy of Jesus Christ. The lion represents Mark, for at the outset of his Gospel is heard the voice of the baptist like that of a lion in the desert. The third, the ox (as sacrificial animal), represents Luke, for he begins with the priest Zechariah. The fourth is the eagle, representing John who lifts himself up on eagle's wings when he speaks of the eternal Word of God."

The four living creatures in the Book of Revelation saw the almighty God sitting on the throne in heaven. The four evangelists, however, tell us how this almighty God entered human history in the person of Jesus of Nazareth. They spell out with narrative detail what during their worship the early Christians confessed in a famous hymn:

The divine likeness was his from the first;
yet he did not think to snatch at equality with God,
but made himself nothing, assuming the nature of a slave.
Bearing the human likeness, revealed in human shape,
he humbled himself, and in obedience accepted even death,
death on the cross.
Therefore God raised him to the heights
and bestowed on him the name above all names,
that at the name of Jesus every knee should bow
—in heaven, on earth, and in the depths—
and every tongue confess, "Jesus Christ is Lord",
to the glory of God the Father (Phil. 2:6–11).

Overtures of oratorios sometimes allude to the major musical themes of the composition. Similarly in the beginning of the four Gospels each evangelist anticipates already the main emphases in his particular testimony.

Plate 1: *East German graphists were asked in 1981 to draw new versions of the traditional symbols for the evangelists for this book. The winning contribution, published as Plate 1, was made by Karl-Heinz Lötzsch, Dresden, GDR.*

It is probable that these introductory passages were written after the whole Gospel had been conceived. The prologues and birth narratives form, in that case, not the first but the last layer of the Gospel tradition. Early Christians confessed first of all the death and resurrection of Christ. Only in the light of the cross, and with the firm belief that the crucified Lord had risen from the dead, did the evangelists deal with the life and ministry of Jesus, beginning with his baptism in the Jordan. The narratives of Jesus' birth in the first two chapters of the Gospels of Matthew and Luke and the prologues to the Gospels of Mark and John function as an overture to the good news of Jesus Christ.

It is essential that the introductions to the Gospels be read as such anticipating overtures. They were written as confessions about Jesus Christ much more than as biographical and historical narratives. No doubt they also contain memories of things which actually happened, yet the point of adding the prologues and the birth stories to the Gospels was to lead readers immediately into theological meditation.

The art work to guide our first meditation (Plate 2) is not a typical Christmas scene. It shows us Christ as the ruler of all. In this miniature from the early Middle Ages, the one who became a vulnerable infant at Bethlehem appears as the Lord of the cosmos. Many centuries before his coming, the prophets—shown here in the medallions—knew already of his coming and pointed to him. The four living creatures surround him with their *Sanctus*. In the corners the four evangelists see, listen and write.

This majestic Christ is the hidden messianic king as *Mark* testifies, the one who walks on God's way, the way to the cross.

He is the Saviour of the world who enters universal history as a little child and thus brings peace to the nations of the whole inhabited world, as is told in *Luke*'s story.

He is the Immanuel who re-enacts the history of the people of Israel by becoming a refugee in Egypt and later a displaced person in Galilee as we meet him in *Matthew*'s account.

According to *John*'s vision he is the Logos, the Word who existed already long before all things were created, who shines as the light which cannot be overcome by darkness.

Each evangelist thus saw, heard and wrote, from his own point of view, about that many-splendoured event of God's coming among us, confessing the Immanuel for different situations of the church in the world. Their testimony about the same mysterious event led to different accents in theology, in the "knowledge and speaking about God".

Through the centuries, Christ's church never ceased to praise this majestic Lord who for our sake humbled himself unto death. The praise is sung not only by the church on earth. It is the ongoing praise of the "host of heaven" in which the faithful join with reverent silence or shouts of joy. One of the earliest great Christian liturgies, that of St James, which was used in the Church of Jerusalem and Syria and the ancient churches in India, contains the following "Cherubic Hymn". The church on earth is here called upon to keep silence and meditate as the heavenly host sings of the mystery of the incarnation:

Let all mortal flesh keep silence
and with fear and trembling stand;
ponder nothing earthly minded,
for with blessing in his hand
Christ our Lord to earth descendeth,
our full homage to demand.

King of kings, yet born of Mary,
as of old on earth he stood,
Lord of lords, in human vesture
—in the Body and the Blood—
he will give to all the faithful
his own Self for heavenly food.

Rank on rank the host of heaven
spreads its vanguard on the way,
as the Light of light descendeth
from the realms of endless day,
that the powers of hell may vanish
as the darkness clears away.

At his feet the six-winged seraph:
cherubim with sleepless eye,
veil their faces to the Presence,
as with ceaseless voice they cry,
"Alleluia, Alleluia,
Alleluia, Lord most high".

Plate 2: *"Majestas Domini", miniature in the Bible of Vivian, Tours/France. Early Middle Ages.*

Mark's Good News

Evangel (*euangelion*)—Gospel—Good News: originally this was not a book but the proclamation of a joyous message. Both in Old Testament times and in the Greek and Roman world in which Mark lived the term "gospel" had this meaning. A messenger comes running from a battle-field or from the capital city, and whenever he meets people he cries: "The victory has been won!", or "A son is born to the king!", or "A new ruler is being enthroned!"

One could thus render the title of Mark's testimony: "Beginning of the herald's announcement of Jesus Christ", or "Beginning of the proclaimed good news about Jesus Christ". In fact, for almost a hundred years Christians were at a loss to find a suitable name for that new type of testimony which Mark and the other evangelists had written. Then, around A.D. 150, Justin Martyr called these novel writings "the evangels", the gospels, and the name stuck.

Mark does indeed start with a messenger. No less than four times in his prologue the evangelist mentions the desert. There John the baptist prepared the way for the expected Messiah. There we meet Jesus tempted and among the wild beasts. It was his description of John the baptist as "a voice crying aloud in the wilderness" which led to the assignment to Mark of the symbol of the roaring lion.

The testimonies of the evangelists were not signed with the writers' names. Nothing in the Gospel states directly that the author was identical with the John Mark mentioned in the Acts and in apostolic letters (e.g. Acts 12:12; 1 Pet. 5:13), as is often assumed. Nor are there any clear indications as to when, where, why and for whom the Gospel was written. The oldest recorded tradition we have comes from Papias, the bishop of Hierapolis (A.D. 130/140): "Mark had become the interpreter of Peter. He accurately wrote down what he remembered of the things said or done by the Lord, though not in order. For he had neither heard the Lord nor been his personal follower. But he followed Peter who used to adapt his teachings to the needs of his hearers."

Some two hundred years later Eusebius, the first church historian, added the following interesting detail: "Those who heard Peter were not satisfied with hearing him only once . . . They pleaded with Mark, a follower of Peter, to leave them a written document about the teachings which they had heard. And they did not cease to insist until he complied with their request. Such was the origin of the written Good News which bears the name of Mark."

Such accounts cannot be taken as historically accurate, but they give us valuable insights into what the evangelists were called upon to do and what in fact they accomplished.

—Mark did not set out to give us an eye-witness account of what exactly happened. Nor did he intend to write a biography of Jesus. Rather, he transmitted the oral testimony of the apostles and the early church about what Jesus had said and done.

—The telling of the story thus preceded the writing. This writing was not meant to replace the continuing proclamation of the good news. On the contrary, it was meant to help people to remember so that they could hear, memorize and tell the story long after the first witnesses had died.

—In telling the good news Peter himself "used to adapt his teachings to the needs of the hearers", as Papias recalls. Following Peter's example, the early church and the evangelists themselves continued to be sensitive to the needs of their hearers and readers. The tradition received from the apostles was transmitted, with new accents for new situations. Mark, like the other evangelists, became not simply a passive transmitter and copier, but in a true sense an "interpreter".

What are the special emphases of Mark's interpretation? What did he testify about the coming of the expected messianic king?

The Mark painted on parchment in an ancient Ethiopian gospel volume (Plate 3) looks straight at us with large questioning eyes. It is as if he were asking us: "Do you know this Jesus about whom I am going to write? Do you understand God's way which Jesus pioneered for you?" It is as if he were telling us: "Read the prologue which I have written, because there you find the clues for the story of Jesus!"

This is what Mark wrote:

1. Here begins the gospel of Jesus Christ the Son of God.
2. In the prophet Isaiah it stands written: "Here is my herald whom I send on ahead of you, and he will
3. prepare your way. A voice crying aloud in the wilderness, 'Prepare a way for the Lord; clear a
4. straight path for him.'" And so it was that John the baptist appeared in the wilderness proclaiming a baptism in token of repentance, for the forgiveness
5. of sins; and they flocked to him from the whole Judaean country-side and the city of Jerusalem, and were baptized by him in the River Jordan, confessing their sins.
6. John was dressed in a rough coat of camel's hair, with a leather belt round his waist, and he fed on
7. locusts and wild honey. His proclamation ran: "After me comes one who is mightier than I. I am
8. not fit to unfasten his shoes. I have baptized you with water; he will baptize you with the Holy Spirit."
9. It happened at this time that Jesus came from Nazareth in Galilee and was baptized in the Jordan by
10. John. At the moment when he came up out of the water, he saw the heavens torn open and the Spirit,
11. like a dove, descending upon him. And a voice spoke from heaven: "You are my Son, my Beloved; on you my favour rests."
12. Thereupon the Spirit sent him away into the
13. wilderness, and there he remained for forty days tempted by Satan. He was among the wild beasts; and the angels waited on him. (Mark 1:1–13).

In his Good News Mark tells us about the way which Jesus had to go. The artist who drew the symbols of the evangelists reproduced in this book, put a cross in the centre of all of them. This is particularly appropriate for Mark's testimony. The Christians among whom this Gospel was written—the church in Rome around A.D. 70?—probably had a one-sided image of Jesus. They saw in him, in the first place, a human miracle-worker of extraordinary powers, and they worshipped him as a divine redeemer without a human face. Mark does not ignore the miracles. In the first half of his Gospel he shows us that Jesus has indeed the power to heal those who believe in him. Nor does Mark deny the centrality of the resurrection. Throughout his Good News he lets us know that in a hidden way Jesus is indeed the Son of God, the expected messianic king who ultimately defeats death and all evil powers. However, Mark corrects a one-sided triumphant under-standing of Jesus. He shows that the hidden king was fully human. He insists that the Messiah had to go the way to the cross. Mark's Good News takes therefore the shape of a passion story with an extended introduction.

Before the curtain rises for the drama of the hidden king's way to the cross, the evangelist sets the stage and presents the main actors. Old Testament prophecies indicate that a new exodus, a new liberation—the salvation story in fact—is about to begin (Mk 1:2–3). Multitudes of people flock to John the baptist in the desert, but as God's herald the baptist directs their attention to the one who is to come (1:4–8). Then the main actor appears. We meet him not yet in his disguise as a rejected Jewish rabbi, but as the one who is God's Son. The divine voice acknowledges: "You are my Son, my Beloved; on you my favour rests" (1:9–11). Immediately comes forth Jesus' opponent, Satan, and the battle is joined in the desert for the symbolic period of forty days (1:12–13).

It is as if the evangelist wants to give the readers some idea of the whole plot before the drama actually begins. Later in the story the disciples appear again and again as men who do not really understand their master, and misinterpret his messiahship. Through his Gospel Mark enables us to perceive who Jesus really is and how we must follow him on the way to the cross.

The evangelist in the painting on the ancient Ethiopian Gospel volume (Plate 3) looks straight at us. His large eyes invite us to learn from his testimony what God's way is which Jesus pioneered for us. The prologue gives us the clue to that testimony.

Plate 3: *Evangelist Mark. Illumination from the Gospel book of Emperor Amda Seyon I (1314–44). Ethiopa. Early 14th century.*

The way of the Lord

We are on the way, as persons, nations, and as the whole of humanity. But what is our goal and how will we endure the dangers of the road?

The old monastic breviary of the Roman Catholic Church contains a blessing for those who embark on a journey. During the late Middle Ages many fervently sought this blessing as they ventured on dangerous roads. This short litany for travellers is almost forgotten today, though seldom we had such need of it as in our own times. It starts with the Benedictus in Luke 1:68–79 which leads up to the request: "Guide our feet into the way of peace!" This request is echoed in the response of the people, and the litany then continues with the following prayer:

Lord, you led the people of Israel with dry feet right through the ocean. By the guidance of the star you showed the three sages the way towards yourself. Give us now a happy journey and peaceful times. Let us safely reach our goal. Accompany us by your holy messengers, that finally we reach the shore of eternal salvation.

Lord, you led your servant Abraham out of Ur, the land of the Chaldeans, and safely guarded him on all the ways of his pilgrimage. Guard us, too, your servants, we pray.

Be our helper, O Lord, as we set out, be comfort on the way, shadow in the heat. Be our roof in rain and frost, our friend when we grow weary, shelter when in danger, support on slippery roads. Be the saving harbour in shipwreck, so that with your guidance we joyfully reach our goal and return to our home without harm.

Almighty God, let your family walk in the path of salvation, we pray. Let them follow the warnings of your forerunner, John the baptist, that they safely come to him whom he announced, to our Lord Jesus Christ, your Son.

The blessing invoked integrates the journey of the travellers into the pilgrimage of God's people in the Old Testament. It thus leads them to John the baptist who points to Jesus. Similarly, Mark's prologue invites the readers to participate with their life's journey in a pilgrimage which started long before they were born. This pilgrimage leads through a desert where the road is still to be built, yet it is the Lord's road. If we walk on it we too will meet John the baptist who points to Jesus.

Two prophecies concerning the Lord's way stand at the beginning of Mark's Gospel:

I am sending my messenger
who will clear a path before me (Mal. 3:1).

Prepare a road for the Lord
through the wilderness,
clear a highway
across the desert for our God (Isa. 40:3).

The first prophecy was spoken by a man who called himself "Malachi", which in Hebrew means "the messenger". In the early fifth century B.C. he addressed the descendants of the Jews who had returned from the exile in Babylon. They were disillusioned despite the fact that the temple had been rebuilt. Doubts assailed them. Was the God of their forefathers, the Lord of judgment and grace, still alive? Malachi's words about God's path echo the message of hope of another prophet. Some seventy years earlier those who had been deported to Babylon were consoled and encouraged by the "Second Isaiah"—so called because his prophecies are collected in the second part of the book of Isaiah (Isa. 40–55). He announced to the exiles a new exodus: just as their forefathers had been liberated from Egypt and led through the desert to Palestine, so they too would soon be liberated from the exile in Babylon and brought back to Jerusalem. Moreover, God himself would return with his people to the promised land.

Even before Mark's time the two prophecies from Second Isaiah and Malachi were probably put together in a collection of prophetic announcements about the expected messianic king. Not God himself but the Messiah would lead the new exodus. As usual in such Jewish and Christian reinterpretations of old prophecies, the biblical text was reworded to suit the new meaning. Mark's quotation thus changes Malachi's prophecy: the messenger is not sent "before me" (i.e. God), but "ahead of you" (i.e. ahead of the messianic king). Consequently the road being prepared is not God's path but the Messiah's way.

A small fresco from the Roman catacombs of Priscilla (Plate 4) is probably the oldest preserved painting which relates to Christ's incarnation. From behind on the left side a man in the form of an ancient orator looks at the scene in the foreground to the right with a mother feeding her child. The infant still holds the mother's breast, but he has turned his head, as if listening to a voice. The "prophet" carries a scroll in his left hand and points with his right towards a star, now only barely visible, above the child. This fresco is part of a larger painted stucco which shows Jesus as the good shepherd, carrying a lamb and standing in the midst of sheep and low flowering trees. The one who was announced by

Plate 4: *Small early Christian fresco on an arch of the Capella Greca in the catacombs of Priscilla, Rome. Usually interpreted as Balaam pointing to the star or Isaiah announcing the birth of Immanuel. First half of 3rd century.*

prophets and who came as an infant is the expected shepherd-king.

Different interpretations have been given of this early Christian painting, and it can in fact shed light on the beginnings of all four Gospels. Usually the man in the background is identified with Balaam, the gentile prophet from the East, who announced that "a star shall come forth out of Jacob, a comet arise from Israel" (Num. 24:17). This Balaam story is probably recalled by Matthew's teaching about the Magi who followed the star from the East and came to Bethlehem where they saw the child with Mary, his mother (Mt. 2:1–12; compare below pp. 73ff).

Others see in this early Christian painting a portrayal of Isaiah 7:14. Around 733 B.C. an army had advanced from the north to lay siege to Jerusalem and put an end to the Davidic dynasty. Then the prophet Isaiah spoke to the frightened king Ahaz: "A young woman is with child, and she will bear a son, and will call him Immanuel" (= "God with us"; Isa. 7:14). Originally this prophecy might have referred to Ahaz' wife and to the birth of Hezekiah, the new Davidic king. Already in the ancient Greek translation of the Old Testament, however, the prophecy had received a wider meaning, and from the second century B.C. onwards it was believed to apply to the birth of the expected messianic king. This is the tradition taken up by the evangelist Matthew (Mt. 1:23) and indirectly by Luke (Lk. 1:26–38).

The Balaam story and the Immanuel prophecy were probably uppermost in the mind of the early Christian artist. However, his painting can also apply to the prologue of John's Gospel. In this case the prophet stands for John the baptist. "He came as a witness to testify to the light . . . He was not himself the light; he came to bear witness to the light. The real light which enlightens every person was even then coming into the world." And—as the prologue of John's Gospel further affirms—this true word and light and life became incarnate, "he came to dwell among us, and we saw his glory, such glory as befits the Father's only Son, full of grace and truth" (Jn 1:6ff, 14).

The painting in the Priscilla catacombs can similarly illuminate Mark's prologue: Malachi and the Second Isaiah speak about a messenger, later identified with Elijah and John the baptist. This messenger prepares the way of the Lord. Yet the Lord is no more the transcendent God of the Old Testament but Jesus of Nazareth who guides his disciples on the way to the cross and to the victory.

Both Mark and the early Christian painter see ancient prophecies fulfilled in the coming of Jesus. This stands in striking contrast to another reading about how to prepare the way for the Lord. A century before Mark wrote, the members of a Jewish sectarian movement quoted Isaiah 40:3 for explaining their retreat into the Judaean desert. They lived as an ascetic community in the forbidding settlement of Qumran, untouched by the corruption of this world and set aside for studying the Jewish scriptures. Thus they hoped to prepare the way for the Lord. Mark too brings us into the Judaean desert where the messenger John baptizes and Jesus is tempted. Yet the way of Christian discipleship which starts from the desert leads to the struggles of faith in the midst of the world's affairs.

The Messianic King

You are my son,
this day I become your father (Ps. 2:7).

Originally such texts merely referred to ruling or newly born Davidic kings. These were the anointed ones, the "messiahs", but in a sense which had not yet acquired the later and fuller meaning of a world saviour. As time went on, as one Davidic king after another fell short of the hopes which were centred in him, the people reread and reinterpreted the old "messianic" texts. Among certain groups of the Jewish people, and at the latest from the 2nd century B.C. onwards, the expectation of the coming of *the* messianic king grew stronger and stronger.

The prophecy of Isaiah 11:1ff was one among the texts now understood as referring to this coming messianic king:

Then a shoot shall grow from the stock of Jesse,
and a branch shall spring from his roots.
The spirit of the Lord shall rest upon him . . .
(Compare also Isa. 42:1ff).

From the early Middle Ages onwards, this prophecy has often been portrayed in Christian art. One of the famous 12th century stained glass windows of the cathedral of Chartres shows an elaborate form of this "Tree of Jesse". Out of the reclining Jesse grows a tree in which appear superimposed one upon another David, Solomon, two other kings, and Mary. On either side stand fourteen prophets announcing the coming messianic king who is enthroned on the top of the tree.

The "Tree of Jesse" in a later miniature (Plate 5) presents a simplified form. Out of the reclining father of David grows a plant in the form of a vine or a tree of life. Mary, in the posture of prayer and presented as a queen, is at the centre. Above her is enthroned Jesus as the Pantocrator, the ruler of all. Mary in the middle expresses medieval spirituality and is drawn from Luke's story rather than Mark's witness to the Christ. Yet Jesus enthroned as the messianic king on the tree of Jesse is a revealing visual interpretation of Mark's testimony.

The title "Son of God" in the first sentence of Mark's Gospel is perhaps a later copier's addition, as it does not appear in some old manuscripts. Nevertheless, the title expresses perfectly well what Mark wants to testify about Jesus, the Messiah.

In three key passages of Mark's Gospel Jesus is declared to be the Son of God. During his baptism God's voice speaks from heaven: "You are my Son, my Beloved; on you my favour rests" (Mk 1:11). This clearly echoes the divine decrees in 2 Samuel 7, Psalm 2 and possibly also Isaiah 42. In Mark's testimony the legitimation and anointment of Jesus takes place between the divine Father and the designated messianic king only. Neither John the baptist nor any other human witness is aware of what happens. Here, as elsewhere, Jesus' messiahship remains hidden from the actors. This messianic "secrecy" is typical of the whole

The messenger in Mark's prologue has only one task: to point towards the one who is to come, preparing his way. But who is he that comes? In their prologues and introductory chapters the four evangelists give different answers.

Mark responds in the most concise way, in the Greek original with four or perhaps two words only: "Jesus Christ, (God's Son)." Nothing is said about the extraordinary conception and birth of the Messiah, as these are told in Matthew's account and Luke's story. Nor does Mark give us a genealogy of Jesus. No explicit comment is made about the cosmic significance of the incarnation of Christ, as in the prologue to John's Gospel. In the shortest way possible Mark simply names the name of the one who comes: "Jesus". He then adds a title: "Christ", which is the Greek translation of the Hebrew word "Messiah", the Anointed One. Some of the oldest manuscripts of Mark 1:1 stop here, omitting the further title "Son of God".

What did Mark want to communicate when he presented Jesus as the Messiah and the Son of God? His testimony can only be rightly understood if the titles "Messiah" and "Son of God" are seen in the context of their Old Testament meaning.

The basic messianic text of the Old Testament is Nathan's prophecy to David in 2 Samuel 7. The anointed king had planned to build a temple for the Ark of God, a house for the Lord. Yet at night the word of the Lord came to Nathan the prophet. It turned the whole plan around: God will build a house for his Anointed, and this divine promise will embrace also a descendant of David:

I will establish his royal throne for ever.
I will be his father,
and he shall be my son (2 Sam. 7:13f).

Similar promises are also found in later prophetic oracles and especially in the royal psalms which were sung at the coronation of Davidic kings. Thus Psalm 2 describes the turmoil of the nations and the conspiracy of their proud rulers "against the Lord and his anointed king". Yet above all such human tumult the Lord sits firmly enthroned in heaven and, having anointed his king on the mountain of Zion, he decrees:

of Mark's Gospel. As soon as people begin to guess who Jesus really is, they are enjoined secrecy, and asked not to tell anybody (Mk 1:24f, 34; 3:11f; 8:30). Indeed, before Jesus had reached the end of his journey, the cross, he cannot be known as the one who he really is, the suffering messianic king. For the readers of Mark's Gospel, however, already in the prologue this messianic identity is disclosed. It becomes further manifest in his baptism.

Later, when for the first time the coming rejection and suffering of the hidden messianic king have been announced (Mk 8:31), three disciples are admitted into Christ's secret. On the mountain of transfiguration Peter, James and John see Jesus in his royal glory. Again the divine voice declares: "This is my Son, my Beloved; listen to him" (Mk 9:7). But it still is no public event. Even these privileged disciples cannot really grasp its significance: they do not understand the vision of Christ's glory and his way to the cross.

Only when, as a helpless prisoner, Jesus is brought before the high priest—soon to be spat upon, tortured and condemned to death—is the question for the first time publicly asked: "Are you the Messiah, the Son of the Blessed One?" (Mk 14:61). Not until after his agony and death on the cross does someone publicly state who Jesus is. Paradoxically, this confession is made neither by the disciples who run away nor by the women who look on from afar. It is a Roman officer, the chief of the execution squad, who exclaims: "Truly, this man was a/the Son of God!" (Mk 15:39).

Some among the crowd had earlier seen in Jesus the son of David, a national messianic king (Mk 10:47f; 11:10). He himself showed that this is a misleading understanding of his messiahship (Mk 12:35ff). In him not simply a descendant of David had come. Out of Jesse, David's father, a *new* branch had sprung, a *new* messianic king, as the "Tree of Jesse" (Plate 5) so graphically shows.

The old Latin hymn "Veni, veni Emmanuel" sums up well what Mark testifies about the one who in Jesus came to the people of Israel and to all the nations of the world:

O come, O come Immanuel,
and ransom captive Israel
that mourns in lonely exile here
until the Son of God appear.
Rejoice! Rejoice! Immanuel
shall come to thee, O Israel.

O come, thou Rod of Jesse, free
thine own from Satan's tyranny.
From depths of hell thy people save
and give them vict'ry o'er the grave.
Rejoice! Rejoice! Immanuel
shall come to thee, O Israel.

O come, thou dayspring, come and cheer
our spirits by thine advent here;
disperse the gloomy shades of night
and death's dark shadows put to flight.
Rejoice! Rejoice! Immanuel
shall come to thee, O Israel.

O come, thou key of David, come
and open wide our heavenly home;
make safe the way that leads on high,
and close the path to misery.
Rejoice! Rejoice! Immanuel
shall come to thee, O Israel.

Plate 5: *"Tree of Jesse", miniature of a Psalterium (University Library in Freiburg im Breisgau). First half of 13th century.*

The heavens torn apart

We cannot see what lies before us,
we have no prophet now;
we have no one who knows
how long this is to last! (Ps. 74:9)

This moving lament comes from a time of deep crisis. It may recall the destruction of Solomon's temple by the Babylonian army in 587 B.C. (compare Ps. 74:1–8 with 2 Kings 25:8–15). More likely it alludes to the chaos following the death of Alexander the Great, when the Seleucid king Antiochus IV desecrated and ransacked the post-exilic temple in 169 B.C. The inter-testamental book of 1 Maccabees describes that period as "a time of great affliction for Israel, worse than any since the day when prophets ceased to appear among them" (1 Macc. 9:27; compare 1 Macc. 1:20–28; 4:38). The Maccabean revolt, beginning in 167 B.C., let for a moment hopes run high, but the situation soon deteriorated in still more violence, repression and despair.

Such was the mood among many Palestinian Jews at the time when Jesus was born. Later the rabbis said: "When Haggai, Zechariah and Malachi, the last prophets, had died, the Holy Spirit disappeared from Israel; only the *bath-qol* (that is the 'daughter of the Voice', a feeble echo of God's word) was still audible to them."

The heavens were closed, the lines of communication cut. Only faint echoes of the Lord who had so forcefully spoken and acted during the history of the people of Israel could now be heard. No wonder that in such times ardent expectations grew. A new type of literature developed in which apocalyptic (= revealing) visions and dreams answered the anxious cry: "How long?" In these visions the present evil age is confronted with the age to come when God alone will rule and heaven—that is, the realm of God's immediate presence—will be open towards the earth. The change from one age to the other was felt to be imminent. All present trials, sufferings and chaos were therefore experienced only as signs of the coming judgment, as birth pangs of God's kingdom in the coming new age. A variety of some-times contradictory messianic expectations expressed themselves in these apocalyptic visions.

It is in this context of apocalyptic crises and expecta-tions that probably Jesus himself, and with him the first

Christians understood, confessed and interpreted the coming of the Immanuel. The description of John the baptist's appearance and the report of Jesus' baptism were consequently phrased in apocalyptic language.

Mark maintains and uses in his prologue this same apocalyptic interpretation for giving his readers an understanding of what really happened when Jesus entered the scene: God's long silence is finally being broken. At last a prophet appears again, but he only points to a mightier one who will baptize not with water but with the Holy Spirit. Then, as Jesus comes up out of the water, he has a vision and receives divine anointment and acknowledgment: "He saw the heavens torn open and the Spirit, like a dove, descending upon him. And a voice spoke from heaven: 'You are my Son, my Beloved; on you my favour rests'" (Mk 1:10f).

A beautiful Jewish apocalyptic text from the first century B.C. describes the coming of a priestly Messiah in similar terms. It is part of the "Testament of Levi", Aramaic fragments of which have been found near the settlement of Qumran in the Judaean desert. Members of this Jewish religious community expressed their hope in a manner similar to the way the early Christians spoke about this hope. Did this Jewish text influence the Gospel accounts of Jesus' baptism? Or was the Testament of Levi later edited in the light of the Gospels? It is more likely that the texts stand indepen-dent of each other, though both use old biblical language and the apocalyptic symbolism which was current at that time.

This is how the Qumranites saw the coming of their priestly Messiah:

Then shall the Lord raise up a new priest.
To him all the words of the Lord shall be revealed,
and he shall execute a righteous judgment
upon the earth for a multitude of days . . .
The heavens shall be opened.
From the temple of glory shall come upon him sanctification
With the Father's voice as from Abraham to Isaac.
And the glory of the Most High shall be uttered over him,
and the spirit of understanding and sanctification shall rest
upon him . . .
In his priesthood the Gentiles shall be multiplied in knowledge
upon the earth,
and enlightened through the grace of the Lord.
In his priesthood shall sin come to an end,
and the lawless shall cease to do evil.
He shall open the gates of paradise,
and shall remove the threatening sword against Adam
(Test. Levi 18:2, 6ff).

In the Caribbean city named after John, San Juan, the baptist stands with the index of his right hand pointing

Plate 6: *"John the baptist", stone statue by the Puerto-Rican sculptor Rafael López del Campo, San Juan, Puerto Rico. Contemporary.*

to what comes from heaven (Plate 6). The massive statue by the Puerto Rican artist Rafael Lopez del Campo is placed between the ocean and a busy highway of the modern city. The waves breaking unceasingly are like a symbol of world history. The rushing cars on the highway express the one-dimensional bustle of our time. Between the two stands the prophet John, pointing to heaven, to the transcendent dimension of life.

In the history of art John the baptist's finger has become famous, especially from Grünewald's painting of the crucifixion on the altar of Isenheim. There the baptist directs our attention with a long index finger to the suffering Jesus on the cross. As an artistic interpretation of Mark's witness to Jesus, and especially of his passion narrative, Grünewald's painting has no equal. With regard to Mark's prologue, however, the statue in San Juan expresses forcibly what the evangelist wants to communicate.

At a time and place where the heavens seem to be closed, when only weak echoes of God's word can still be heard, suddenly a lonely figure appears. A prophet comes when prophecy seems to have come to an end. A voice, crying in the desert, be it the empty wilderness near the Jordan river or the all-too-noisy asphalt desert of modern cities.

This voice prepares the way for him through whom God will bring about the change from the old to the new age. After this turning point in world history life need no longer be one-dimensional, like the waves driven by the winds to break on the shores, like the city traffic hurrying towards ephemeral goals. Life can now be directed by God's Spirit, because God's presence, the open heaven, surrounds it. On this threshold of the new age the prophet prepares the way for him who will baptize us with the Holy Spirit. More than that he cannot do or see.

Yet in his baptism Jesus steps beyond the threshold and he sees the heavens torn apart! In the accounts of Matthew and Luke one finds the common apocalyptic expression "the heaven opened". Mark uses a more dramatic verb: "The heavens are torn apart." Jesus' vision is like the answer to the passionate question which an Israelite addressed to the God who had for so long been absent, a silent God from afar: "Why did you not rend the heavens and come down, and make the mountains shudder before you?" (Isa. 64:1).

Only one more time does Mark use the same verb in his Gospel. When Jesus had died on the cross "the curtain of the temple was torn in two from top to bottom" (Mk 15:38). In both cases Mark's witness points in the same direction. Through the coming of Jesus as the messianic king and as the suffering Messiah the old separation between heaven and earth, the holy and the common, is abolished. A theophany takes place, God appears among us. The Immanuel has come.

In the fourth Gospel this testimony is emphasized even more strongly. Jesus there testifies about himself: "In truth, in very truth I tell you all, you shall see heaven wide open, and God's angels ascending and descending upon the Son of Man" (Jn 1:51). This saying recalls the famous dream of Jacob: the ladder reaching up to heaven with the angels going up and down. There also a theophany happened, for "the Lord was standing beside him". When Jacob awoke from his sleep he was afraid and said: "How fearsome is this place! This is no other than the house of God, this is the gate of heaven. Therefore Jacob called that place Beth-El, that is the house of God" (Gen. 28:10–22).

Mark may not have intended to make this connection between Jesus' baptism and Jacob's dream. It nevertheless is in line with his prologue if we recognize that Beth-El now remains not a place only, but becomes a person. Having seen the heavens torn apart, received the anointment of the Spirit, and having been acknowledged as the Son of God, Jesus is Beth-El, the gate of heaven.

The fiery wheel

*The chariot wheels of God
are rolling, rolling, rolling on.
And you my brethren who became the victims
of oppression, injustice and cruelty
Weep not any more,
for the chariot wheels of God
are rolling, rolling, rolling over,
and they are here already.*

These are the words of a modern revolutionary song, freely translated from Telugu, an Indian language. Solomon Raj, who made the batik reproduced in Plate 7, writes about it: "This song spoke to my heart, although my concept of God's justice is not just like the mechanical wheel of Karma" (that is the inexorable cycle of birth and death, existence interminably following existence, as reward or punishment). "Nor does it speak to me simply about the overthrow of the present order. I see in it rather the wheel of judgment and hope, the purposeful act of the God of mercy and righteousness. The hand of God reaches out of the cloud and sets the wheel in motion. The prophet points to this from the river of mercy where he proclaims a baptism of repentance for the forgiveness of sins."

It may appear strange to modern readers to relate Mark's prologue to a fiery wheel. Yet there can hardly be found a better symbol for expressing what happened when John the baptist appeared. Jewish readers of the time of Jesus would have immediately made the connection between the wheel of fire and the prophet Elijah. And in doing so they would have discovered the whole point of the first half of Mark's prologue (Mk 1:1–8).

During the centuries immediately before and after Christ, the prophet Elijah played an important role in Jewish expectations. Elijah did not die, he was taken up into heaven. It happened when his disciple Elisha and he had gone across the Jordan: "Suddenly there appeared chariots of fire and horses of fire, which separated them one from the other, and Elijah was carried up in the whirlwind to heaven" (2 Kings 2:11). This same Elijah would return before the final judgment, as the prophet Malachi (or possibly a later addition to this prophetic book) foretells: "Look, I will send you the prophet Elijah before the great and terrible day of the Lord comes. He will reconcile fathers to sons and sons to fathers, lest I come and put the land under a ban to destroy it" (Mal. 4:5f).

The return of Elijah! Many Jews longed for his coming. Would he be the messianic forerunner of God, preparing God's way? Might he possibly be the Messiah himself, the high priest of the close of times? Or will his return point to the coming of the Messiah? Very different expectations did indeed centre around the prophet who was carried up to heaven in a fiery whirlwind.

In the "Wisdom of Sirach", a book of Jewish spirituality from the second century B.C., we have a glowing account of Elijah's work. It sums up the feats of the prophet (as told in 1 Kings 17–21; 2 Kings 1–2; 2 Chron. 21:12ff) and the later expectations concerning him:

*Elijah appeared, a prophet like fire,
whose word flamed like a torch.
He brought famine upon them,
and his zeal made their numbers small.
By the word of the Lord he shut up the sky
and three times called down fire.
How glorious you were, Elijah, in your miracles!
Who else can boast such deeds?
You raised a corpse from death
and from the grave, by the word of the Most High.
You sent kings and famous men
from their sick-beds down to their deaths.
You heard a denunciation at Sinai,
a sentence of doom at Horeb.
So you anointed kings for vengeance,
and prophets to succeed you.
You were taken up to heaven in a fiery whirlwind,
in a chariot drawn up by horses of fire.
It is written that you are to come
at the appointed time with warnings,
to allay the divine wrath before its final fury,
to reconcile father and son,
and to restore the tribes of Jacob.
Happy are those who saw you
and were honoured with your love!* (Sir. 48:1–11)

In his prologue Mark lets discerning readers discover that Elijah did indeed come when John the baptist appeared. Yet the fiery wheel is not Elijah's wagon, it is the Messiah's baptism with the Holy Spirit.

In an overture, the coming melodies are only alluded to, not fully played. Similarly in Mark's prologue, the "messianic" figure of the returning Elijah is not mentioned by name, only referred to by a series of allusions.

The good news of Jesus Christ begins, according to Mark, with the appearance of the baptist who fulfills Elijah's "messianic" role (compare in contrast to this Lk. 16:16 where the baptist still belongs to the period of the law before the gospel). What Mark reports about this John/Elijah (Mk 1:4–8) is the historical realization of the prophetic announcement in verse 2: "Here is my herald whom I send on ahead of you." This quotation from Malachi 3:1 had long before Jesus been understood in the light of the promise that Elijah would return (Mal. 4:5; see above pp. 10ff).

John the baptist begins his ministry in the desert, probably east of the Jordan, where Elijah had been taken up into heaven (2 Kings 2:11; John 1:28). How he is clothed and what he eats are specified, while elsewhere in the New Testament there are no such descriptions. They must have had a special significance for the early Christians and for Mark. Not only is the baptist thereby characterized as a beduin living in the desert as well as a prophet (compare Zech. 13:4), the reference to the "leather belt/apron round his waist" relates him to Elijah (Mk 1:6; 2 Kings 1:8).

The appearance of a messenger in the desert, for early Christians, would be a reminder of the great acts which God accomplished in the desert, especially during the exodus. The reference to Malachi 3:1 is in fact a mixed quotation, recalling also God's promise to the people of Israel during their desert-journey: "Now I send an angel/messenger before you to guard you on your way and to bring you to the place I have prepared. Take heed of him and listen to his voice" (Ex. 23:20f). This applies also to the ministry of John/Elijah.

While Matthew and Luke report the content of the baptist's proclamation (Mt. 3:7–12; Lk. 3:7–17), Mark strictly limits himself to the baptist's function as the one who prepares the Messiah's way. Both the enormous difference and the intimate relationship between the messianic herald and the Messiah himself are emphasized.

On the one hand the baptist/Elijah testifies that he is not even fit to render the typical slave's service to the mighty one who is to come—to bow down and unfasten his shoes. He sharply distinguishes the water baptism he administers, which seals the forgiveness of sins to those who repent, from the coming baptism with the Holy Spirit, which refers to an event of the end of times (compare Joel 2:28f).

On the other hand Mark insists that the coming messianic king and his herald John/Elijah together form the beginning of the good news. Both proclaim repentance, in the context of the imminent messianic age. Moreover, John/Elijah prefigures the destiny of the Messiah. According to Matthew and Luke—and in line with the traditional expectation of the returning Elijah's functions—the baptist announces fierce judgment, and points to the mightier one who would come to "baptize with the Holy Spirit and with fire" (Mt. 3:11; Lk. 3:16). Mark leaves out of his prologue both the judgment and the fire. The messianic king comes to liberate and save. This inevitably includes judgment, yet the accent lies on the good news for those who repent. Hence the Messiah's herald cannot be portrayed as a prophet of doom.

Mark thus assimilates the messianic messenger to the Messiah of his Gospel. Just as the disciples of the suffering Christ will have to follow their master on his way to the cross (Mk 8:34ff), so the forerunner John/Elijah also had to prefigure the Messiah's way: he suffers and dies for his testimony (Mk 1:14; 6:14–29). Jesus himself explained this to his disciples on his way down from the mountain of transfiguration (Mk 9:11–13).

The fiery wheel to which John/Elijah points from the waters of Jordan is not the fire of God's judgment. It symbolizes the baptism of the Holy Spirit, the purifying fire, which can be given only by the one who takes judgment upon himself. The new life he gives comes from his own baptism of blood (Mk 10:38–45), from the final victory won on the cross.

Plate 7: *"The fiery wheel", batik, made for this book by the Indian artist Solomon Raj. 1980.*

The great awaiting

Can we trust Mark's testimony?

Such enormous claims are made for Jesus. Not simply a great man, the founder of a religion, has come in the person of that rabbi from Nazareth. According to Mark's witness God's way can now be known and followed because Jesus became the pioneer on this way. The expected new branch from Jesse, the messianic king, God's own son, has appeared. Even the heavens are torn apart for him, so that he can initiate the new age of God's presence among us. Heralded by Elijah who reappeared in John the baptist, the Mighty One has come, and against him not even Satan can prevail.

Such is the good news to which Mark witnesses in his prologue. Can we trust the truth of such a testimony?

That is no rhetorical question. Even the one most intimately involved in this good news, John the baptist, had his doubts; he sent his disciples to ask Jesus: "Are you the one who is to come, or are we to expect some other?" (Mt. 11:3; Lk. 7:19). Though Mark did not report this enquiry by the baptist, the doubts were real, and they have not become any less real in succeeding centuries.

Even today there stands the "cup of Elijah" on the table of each orthodox Jewish family during the Passover meal. When the meal comes to its end the cup of Elijah is filled with wine, the family rises from their seats and the door of the room or house is opened. This symbolic act relates to the ancient Jewish expectation, that Elijah, the messianic messenger, will return on a Passover night. Sometimes the faithful Jews then sing the song of the martyrs in which they confess: "I believe with perfect faith in the coming of the Messiah, and though he tarry, nevertheless, I do believe!"

The vast majority of the people from among whom Jesus came still wait for the returning Elijah and the coming Messiah. Millions of people have never heard the testimony of Mark, or they have consciously rejected it. Moreover, even Christian believers—including the writer of this book—often ask with the baptist, secretly or openly: "Are you the one who is to come, or are we to expect some other?"

For such doubts and wavering questions Mark might have had more sympathy than we expect. Did he not report to us again and again how even the disciples of Jesus were blind to their master's messiahship? And when finally they seemed to understand, they still misunderstood (Mk 8:27–33). In the hour of truth they slept; all of them fled; one of them betrayed the Messiah; the spokesman of the disciples denied him. None of them was there when he died on the cross (Mk 14:32–50, 66–72; 15:20–39). Some women looked from afar. Even those closest to him did not understand what really happened when the suffering Messiah died. A most unlikely outsider, a Roman army officer, had the first glimpse of what the event meant (Mk 15:39–41).

According to one of the several later additions to Mark's Gospel a woman became the first witness to Jesus' resurrection. This same account reports that the risen Lord appeared to the eleven disciples "and reproached them for their incredulity and dullness, because they had not believed those who had seen him after he was raised from the dead. Then he said to them: 'Go forth to every part of the world, and proclaim the good news to the whole creation'" (Mk 16:9–15). Despite the believers' doubts and misunderstandings, unbelief and dullness, they are called into a universal mission!

Mark's prologue anticipates this cosmic testimony: "*all* of the Judaean country-side and *all* Jerusalemites came out" to the messianic herald John/Elijah (Mk 1:5). During his way on earth Jesus remained the hidden Messiah. Even his followers failed to recognize him. But the time will come when all nations finally know and confess the messianic king in his reign.

"Okoné!" In the language of the Amerindians in Suriname this call means "Come!" It is the title of the large sculpture reproduced in Plate 8 which the Surinamese-Chinese artist Paul Woei has cut out of ebony wood. The Amerindian tribes living in the swamps and jungles of Northern Latin America are a courageous people with a passion for liberty, yet many of their tribes have already disappeared or are now threatened with extinction. Paul Woei has lived among them and become the interpreter of their joys and sorrows, their wisdom of life and their great longing.

Out of the dark jungle with all its fearful natural and spiritual powers this Amerindian woman looks at the light which both intrigues and fascinates her. It is not with a cry, it is almost in a whisper that she says, "Okoné!", "Come!"

In a Venezuelan Christmas carol the call is much more explicit;

Come, O come, long expected Jesus,
Come and dwell with us. Come Lord!
Come, open the portals of your kingdom,
Lord!

Plate 8: *"Okoné!", "Come!" Ebony wood sculpture by the Surinamese-Chinese artist Paul Woei. Contemporary.*

The evangelist Mark knew nothing about the populations in Latin America and their great longing. Nevertheless, the coming of the messianic king for him had a significance far beyond the fate of the Jewish people and the scope of the Palestinian scene. The divine voice which acknowledged and legitimized Jesus as God's son came from the Creator of all things, the Lord over all nations (Ps. 2). Anointed and empowered by God's Spirit, Jesus is immediately sent by this Spirit into the desert for the decisive battle: "and there he remained for forty days tempted by Satan" (Mk 1:13), a testing which recalls the forty days and nights which Moses and Elijah spent in the desert (Ex. 34:28; Deut. 9:18; 1 Kings 19:8). Biblical associations reach further back as one continues to read Mark's testimony: "He was among wild beasts; and the angels waited on him" (Mk 1:13). Beyond Elijah and Moses one is reminded of Adam at the dawn of time.

Adam and Eve were tested and tempted, and they failed. Therefore they lost the intimate contact with their Creator and all of God's creatures. The gates of paradise were closed behind them. In the "Testament of Naphthali", a Jewish apocalyptic writing from the 2nd or 1st century B.C., the following promise for the end of times is made to those who are righteous:

Both men and angels shall bless you;
and God shall be glorified among the Gentiles through you,
and the devil shall flee from you,
and the wild beasts shall fear you,
and the Lord shall love you,
and the angels shall cleave to you (Test. Naphthl. 8:4).

In Jesus the righteous one has appeared, the messianic king who is mightier than satan. As the new Adam he restores the relationship of love; with God, with his creation and among his creatures (compare Isa. 11:6–10).

Those who believe that the Creator of all things and the Lord over all history has indeed come among us in Christ Jesus must turn away from their gods and idols. A painful conversion must happen, when we commit ourselves to the good news. Something of that process of conversion, full of awe and expectancy, is expressed in Paul Woei's sculpture. The Amerindian woman has as yet only turned her head and not her body and the position of her feet in the direction of the light.

Another moving expression of what happens when Christ enters one's life and culture is expressed in the poem "Last word from the Tongan Gods" by Siosaia Folau, an inhabitant of the Tongan islands kingdom in the Pacific Ocean. The poem starts with the beating of the Lali, the large Tongan drum, by which the Tongan gods gather all the people to thank them for all the worship, sacrifices and feasts received, and to bid them farewell. Yet the people protest and call on their gods:

Tangaloa, Mani, Hikule'o, wait a minute.
Thank you for the land you provide,
thank you for healing our sickness,
for protection and your guidance.
We know you right from the beginning
through stones, trees, fish and all creation.
But what else can we give
so that you never take your leave?

Then the speaker among the Tongan gods responds:

I smell somebody is coming.
He seems to be a Mighty One.
He can take all my responsibilities.
He loves you more than I do.
I provide you with everything, not my life.
He gives you everything, even his life.
I know who I am:
A messenger of the Mighty One.

Luke's story

1.

26. In the sixth month the angel Gabriel was sent from
27. God to a town in Galilee called Nazareth, with a message for a girl betrothed to a man named Joseph, a descendant of David; the girl's name was
28. Mary. The angel went in and said to her, "Greetings,
29. most favoured one! The Lord is with you." But she was deeply troubled by what he said and wondered
30. what this greeting might mean. Then the angel said to her, "Do not be afraid, Mary, for God has been
31. gracious to you; you shall conceive and bear a son,
32. and you shall give him the name Jesus. He will be great; he will bear the title 'Son of the Most High'; the Lord God will give him the throne of his ancestor
33. David, and he will be king over Israel for ever; his
34. reign shall never end." "How can this be?" said Mary;
35. "I am still a virgin." The angel answered, "The Holy Spirit will come upon you, and the power of the Most High will overshadow you; and for that reason
36. the holy child to be born will be called 'Son of God'. Moreover your kinswoman Elizabeth has herself conceived a son in her old age; and she who is reputed barren is now in her sixth month, for God's
37. promises can never fail." "Here am I," said Mary; "I
38. am the Lord's servant; as you have spoken, so be it." Then the angel left her.

2.

1. In those days a decree was issued by the Emperor Augustus for a registration to be made throughout
2. the Roman world. This was the first registration of its kind; it took place when Quirinius was governor
3. of Syria. For this purpose everyone made his way to
4. his own town; and so Joseph went up to Judaea from
5. the town of Nazareth in Galilee, to register at the city of David, called Bethlehem, because he was of the house of David by descent; and with him went Mary
6. who was betrothed to him. She was expecting a child, and while they were there the time came for
7. her baby to be born, and she gave birth to a son, her first-born. She wrapped him in his swaddling clothes, and laid him in a manger, because there was no room for them to lodge in the house.
8. Now in this same district there were shepherds out in the fields, keeping watch through the night over
9. their flock, when suddenly there stood before them an angel of the Lord, and the splendour of the Lord
10. shone round them. They were terror-stricken, but the angel said, "Do not be afraid; I have good news for you: there is great joy coming to the whole
11. people. Today in the city of David a deliverer has
12. been born to you—the Messiah, the Lord. And this is your sign: you will find a baby lying wrapped in
13. his swaddling clothes, in a manger." All at once there was with the angel a great company of the heavenly host, singing the praises of God:
14. "Glory to God in highest heaven, and on earth his peace for men on whom his favour rests."
15. After the angels had left them and gone into heaven the shepherds said to one another, "Come, we must go straight to Bethlehem and see this thing that has happened, which the Lord has made known
16. to us." So they went with all speed and found their way to Mary and Joseph; and the baby was lying in
17. the manger. When they saw him, they recounted
18. what they had been told about this child; and all who
19. heard were astonished at what the shepherds said. But Mary treasured up all these things and pondered
20. over them. Meanwhile the shepherds returned glorifying and praising God for what they had heard and seen; it had all happened as they had been told.

Luke 1:26–38; 2:1–20

Luke begins his story about Jesus Christ in the temple of Jerusalem—the reason why the ox, as a sacrificial animal, became the symbol of the evangelist. While offering incense in the sanctuary the priest Zechariah sees in a vision the angel Gabriel who announces the birth of John the baptist. Because of his disbelief Zechariah is struck dumb. Leaving the sanctuary, he cannot pronounce the blessing over the worshippers assembled in the temple court. Luke reports: "The people were waiting for Zechariah, surprised that he was staying so long inside. When he did come out he could not speak to them, and they realized that he had had a vision in the sanctuary. He stood there making signs to them, and remained dumb" (Lk. 1:21f).

This liturgical setting is typical of Luke's testimony. A striking miniature in king Otto III's gospel book (ca. A.D. 1000) presents Luke as a great visionary. With upraised arms he carries like Atlas the heavens, symbolized by the cloud of God's presence. Lightnings issue from the cloud where, besides the symbolic ox, one sees angels, king David and other prophetic figures from the Old Testament. The unknown painter of this miniature must have meditated on the first two chapters of Luke's Gospel. Indeed, throughout the childhood narratives about both John the baptist and Jesus one sees heavenly messengers, powers and light appearing on the earthly scene from above. The human actors—Zechariah, Elisabeth, Mary, the shepherds, Simeon and Hannah—are all portrayed with characteristic Old Testament features. On the lower, earthly scene they respond to the interventions from the heavenly scene with prayers full of allusions to Old Testament hymns and prophecies.

At the end of the first volume of his Gospel Luke returns to the liturgical setting. After his death and resurrection Jesus led the disciples out of Jerusalem, "and blessed them with uplifted hands; and in the act of blessing he parted from them and was carried up into heaven" (Lk. 24:50f). The unfinished worship service at the beginning of the Gospel is now being completed, but the blessing no more falls on the Jews alone gathered in the temple court. The whole oikoumene, the whole inhabited world becomes a temple court, where all nations hear the good news and respond with conversion and joy. Therefore Luke—and he alone among the evangelists—wrote after the first a second volume of his Gospel: after the Acts of the earthly Jesus comes the so-called Acts of the Apostles which could better be called the Acts of the heavenly Jesus through God's Spirit and the church.

Luke made "an orderly account", "a connected narrative" of the gospel traditions which had been "handed down to us by the original eye-witnesses and servants of the gospel" (Lk. 1:1–4). After the introductory chapters he first tells how Jesus was empowered at baptism by the Spirit and—filled with this Spirit—accomplished mighty acts and taught with authority in Galilee (Lk. 3–9:50). Then follows the narrative account of the journey from Galilee to Jerusalem during which Jesus instructed his disciples and challenged the people of Israel (Lk. 9:51–19:27). The third part contains the report and interpretation of what happened in Jerusalem, when Jesus was crucified and rose from the dead (Lk. 19:28–24:53).

At the conclusion of his first volume Luke leads the readers back into the temple. After the ascension of their Lord the disciples "returned to Jerusalem with great joy, and spent all their time in the temple praising God" (Lk. 24:52f). They had to wait until they also would be empowered by the Spirit (Lk. 24:49; Acts 1:8).

The second volume of Luke's Gospel opens with a new account of the ascension. Then—after Pentecost—the blessing of the ascending Lord escalates from Jerusalem to Judaea, Samaria, Antioch, Athens and Rome, to the ends of the earth. At the end of Acts Luke therefore portrays the prisoner Paul confidently declaring to the Jewish leaders in Rome: "Take notice that this salvation of God has been sent to the Gentiles; the Gentiles will listen!" (Acts 28:28).

Plate 9: *"Saint Luke painting the madonna", by the Flemish painter Rogier van der Weyden (1435–40). Alte Pinakothek, Munich.*

Who was this Luke who wrote such an artfully constructed history of salvation in two volumes? Luke tells us nothing about himself. Nor do we know anything about Theophilus, to whom the evangelist dedicated the two books.

From the end of the 2nd century onwards the evangelist was identified with the physician Luke who is mentioned three times in the New Testament letters as a companion of Paul. However that may be—good reasons for and against this assumption have been put forward—Luke was certainly not an eye-witness of the earthly Jesus. He probably wrote some time between A.D. 75 and 90. Presumably a gentile Christian himself, he addressed his testimony to a predominantly gentile church, perhaps one issuing from Paul's missionary work. He must have had access to Mark's Gospel and a collection of sayings of Jesus which was known also to Matthew. In addition he had collected traditions about Jesus not known to other evangelists, though John sometimes used similar information. Above all, the evangelist had thoroughly studied the Greek translation of the Old Testament.

In his two-volume Gospel Luke demonstrates that within God's plan of salvation the period of Jesus and the subsequent period of the universal church are fully in line with the period of the history of Israel. It is in the temple that Simeon, a prophetic Jew, recognizes Jesus as a light to the Gentiles, as the glory of God's people Israel (Lk. 2:32). Thus world history, with actors like Augustus and other Roman emperors, becomes the scene of the history of salvation (Lk. 2:1; 3:1; Acts 25:12). And unlike Matthew, who traces Jesus' genealogy from Abraham downwards to Joseph and Mary, Luke gives us a genealogy which starts from Jesus, "the son, as people thought, of Joseph" and which goes back beyond the Israelite patriarchs to "Adam, son of God" (Lk. 3:23, 38).

Luke knew the Greek language better than the other evangelists. He had great gifts as a story-teller, and he could adapt his style to the particular situation and incident on which he wrote. With a few striking details he could portray a person or a situation in such a way that they stick in the memory. It is therefore not astonishing that from the 6th century onwards a legend began to circulate which presented Luke as a painter. From the point of view of history this is not accurate, but as a description of Luke the legend contains much truth.

Especially in the introductory chapters Luke "paints" Mary and the child with loving respect. We can well imagine him kneeling, as Rogier van der Weyden portrays him in his painting (Plate 9). The scene is intimate, and at the same time opens up ever widening horizons. Mary has no halo and the evangelist's symbol of the ox does not appear. The symbolic allusions to the great truths of faith, typical for eastern iconography and early medieval art, have been replaced by a love for details which are realistically drawn. The incarnation takes place in the midst of ordinary history. This is characteristic not only of van der Weyden's painting but also of the evangelist Luke; he testifies to Jesus with stories rather than theological reflections.

The annunciation to Mary (Lk. 1:26–38) and the adoration of the new-born child (Lk. 2:1–20) will be the subjects for the following meditations. Before turning to these two scenes from the childhood narratives it is helpful to survey the two introductory chapters as a whole. Nothing is told there about the Magi or the flight to Egypt. Herod is mentioned only in passing, and Joseph plays no important role. Luke's introduction is marked by three elements.

First, Jesus and John the baptist are set side by side. There are two annunciations of their conception (Lk. 1:5–25 and 1:26–38), complemented by the meeting of the two expectant mothers (Lk. 1:39–56). There are two accounts of the birth, circumcision, naming and predictions of future greatness of the baptist and of Jesus (Lk. 1:57–80 and Lk. 2:1–40), complemented by the scene with the twelve-year old Jesus among the scribes in the temple (Lk. 2:41–52). In all these juxtapositions the precedence of Jesus is consistently emphasized.

Secondly, these narratives contain several hymns of adoration which recall many Old Testament affirmations and thereby interpret the meaning of what is said. The most outstanding are the Magnificat by Mary (Lk. 1:46–55), the Benedictus by Zechariah (Lk. 1:68–79), the Gloria of the heavenly host (Lk. 2:14) and the Nunc Dimittis by Simeon (Lk. 2:29–32). The messages of annunciation (Lk. 1:13–17, 30–33) also include such hymnic material.

Thirdly, the infancy narratives are closer to the Book of Acts than to the first volume of Luke's Gospel. Just as the church after Pentecost becomes an instrument of the Holy Spirit, John the baptist, Mary, Elisabeth, Zechariah and Simeon are moved to act and speak by the power of the Spirit (Lk. 1:15, 35, 41, 67, 80; 2:25–27). Luke's overture to his two-volume gospel "symphony" anticipates what later the church discovered gradually under the guidance of the Spirit.

Ave Maria

Ave Maria, gratia plena!

Hail, O favoured one,
the Lord is with you.

There are few passages in the Bible which have inspired more fervent prayer than this announcement of the angel Gabriel to Mary:

Do not be afraid, Mary,
for God has been gracious to you.
You shall conceive and bear a son,
and you shall give him the name Jesus.
He will be great;
he will bear the title "Son of the Most High".
The Lord God will give him the throne
*   of his ancestor David,*
and he will be king over Israel for ever,
His reign shall never end (Lk. 1:28–33).

Later this announcement will be set in its biblical context (see below, pp. 32ff). We shall examine which Old Testament texts find an echo in Gabriel's words, which Old Testament figures foreshadow Mary and how Luke communicates the good news about Jesus Christ by telling the story of the annunciation.

The history of piety, however, cannot be ignored, especially with a text which has played such a crucial role in it. In this first meditation on the annunciation we shall therefore try to see how in a given time and place the Christian church had understood these words addressed to Mary.

The hymn "Ave maris stella" has been sung in the Western church since the ninth century and it expresses well the place Mary received throughout the Middle Ages.

Star of sea and ocean
gateway to man's heaven
mother of our Maker
hear our pray'r, O Maiden.

Welcoming the Ave
of God's simple greeting
you have borne a Saviour
far beyond all dreaming.

Loose the bonds that hold us
bound in sin's own blindness
that with eyes now open'd
God's own light may guide us.

Show yourself our mother
he will hear your pleading
whom your womb has sheltered
and whose hand brings healing.

Gentlest of all virgins,
that our love be faithful
keep us from all evil
gentle, strong and grateful.

Guard us through life's dangers
never turn and leave us
may our hope find harbour
in the calm of Jesus.

Sing to God our Father
through the Son who saves us
joyful in the Spirit
everlasting praises.

A late medieval visual interpretation of such piety centred on Mary can be seen on the first page of the *Biblia pauperum.*

The "Bibles of the poor" originated from a Benedictine source in Austria or south-east Germany. Since A.D. 1300 copies of these ingenious pictorial summaries of the biblical testimony began to circulate, serving in the first place poor and itinerant clergy (the *pauperes*) as tools for teaching and preaching. The central image of each lesson shows an event of salvation, almost always a scene from Jesus' life and ministry. It is surrounded by four prophetic figures who prophesy what happens. In addition, each of the central New Testament events is in a typological way interpreted by two episodes from the Old Testament. Corresponding titles and short explanatory texts in Latin or German complete the teaching. Those who memorized the visual lessons—originally not more than thirty-four—began to see the inner relationships between the two Testaments. The theology of the *Biblia pauperum* may not appeal to us today, but its biblical pedagogy remains excellent.

Plate 10 reproduces the first page in the relatively late Heidelberg manuscript of the *Biblia pauperum*. The annunciation to Mary appears as the central image, surrounded on each side by two prophets. Above it two Old Testament scenes prefigure, in a negative and positive way, what happened when Gabriel visited Mary.

The first Old Testament type for the annunciation is God's curse on the snake (Gen. 3). The old sequence of perdition starts with the temptation by Satan, leading to doubt, disobedience and sin, to which Eve and Adam yielded. This foreshadows as a contrast the new sequence of the salvation. It begins with the announcement by

Gabriel, leading to faith, commitment and the virginal conception by Mary. In the story of the fall God expelled Eve and Adam from paradise because of their disobedience. In the story of the annunciation God's plan of salvation is made possible by Mary's consent. Eve's name is turned around: the EVA becomes the AVE addressed to Mary. Medieval religious poetry describes Mary therefore as the "gate of paradise".

The second Old Testament type portrays the scene when the angel of the Lord came to Gideon with the message: "You are a brave man, and the Lord is with you", calling him to save the Israelites from the oppression of the Midianites by the power of God's Spirit. Gideon is given the sign of the fleece which was soaked with dew while all the surrounding ground remained dry (Judges 6:12, 36ff). Church fathers saw in this drenched fleece a symbol for the church, but in medieval theology it was interpreted to signify Mary. Thus Honorius of Augustodunum wrote in the twelfth century: "The fleece soaked with dew is our holy Lady blessed with a child; the dry earth around it is her uninjured virginity."

The prophets around the main image are David, Isaiah, Jeremiah and Ezekiel (in the Heidelberg manuscript the last two have been inversed, assigning to Jeremiah a prophecy of Ezekiel and vice versa). David quotes Psalm 72:6, understood here as an allusion to the Gideon episode and its application to Mary. Isaiah contributes his famous Immanuel prophecy (Isa. 7:14). Ezekiel refers to his vision of the eastern gate of the new Temple through which only God has entered and which must remain closed for human passage (Ez. 44:1–3);

from ancient church fathers onwards this text was interpreted as a pointer to the mystery of virginal conception. Jerome (†420) explained in a similar way the enigmatic prophecy of Jeremiah: "The Lord has created a new thing on earth: a woman surrounds a man" (literal translation of Jer. 31:22).

In the portrayal of the annunciation itself the angel Gabriel repeats the gesture of God's right hand. He is shown as the fully representative divine messenger. Mary looks up from the Holy Scripture on which she is meditating. As the mother of him who will be given the throne of king David she herself sits on a throne. "God is with you!" In the twelfth century, Bernard of Clairvaux had interpreted this message in a trinitarian way, and the painter gives us a visual translation of this threefold meaning:

With you is not only the Lord,
the Son whom you clothe with flesh,
but also the Lord,
the Holy Spirit whom you receive,
and the Lord,
the Father who has begotten the one you conceive.
The Father is with you,
who makes his Son also yours.
The Son is with you
to accomplish in you a great mystery:
miraculously opening in you the place of incarnation
and preserving for you the seal of virginity.
The Holy Spirit is with you,
who together with the Father and the Son
makes your womb a sanctuary.
Thus the Lord is with you.

Plate 10: *"Annunciation", Heidelberg manuscript of* Biblia pauperum. *First half of 15th century.*

Da chündet der engel vnser frawen

Dauid

ysaias

Er wirt ab gnad als

Es wirt ein magt ein

Aue maria plena domini

er regt in den

pfaher vnd aine

Jeremias

Ezechiel

Das tor wirt beslozē

Got wirt ein newr

vō hertzen

diuch tün auf der

The power of the Most High

Mary in William Congdon's Annunciation (Plate 11) is invaded from above by the Spirit. It is as if a fire falls from heaven to consume her. Yet she makes no gesture of defence and self-preservation.

According to Luke's account Mary simply asks an astonished question after the announcement that she would conceive and bear a son: "How can this be? I am still a virgin" (Lk. 1:34). The answer she receives is full of allusions to God's action in the Old and the New Testament. "The Holy Spirit will come upon you, and the power of the Most High will overshadow you; and for that reason the holy child to be born will be called 'Son of God' " (Lk. 1:35).

In dealing with Mark's prologue, we looked at some of the biblical key passages about the "Son of God" (see above pp. 13ff). This title designates Jesus first of all as the messianic king, the root of Jesse. In Mark's testimony nothing is said about God engendering Jesus or Mary conceiving by the power of the Holy Spirit. There, after his baptism, Jesus is acknowledged and legitimized as God's son. His sonship is not explained but confessed: "Truly, this man was a/the Son of God" (Mk 15:39).

In Luke's Gospel the title "Son of God" receives a more literal meaning than in Mark's testimony, and the annunciation story begins to explain how Jesus came into that unique relationship with his divine father.

"The Holy Spirit will come upon you, and the power of the Most High will overshadow you." The verb "to overshadow" brings forth important biblical echoes. During the exodus the cloud of God's presence overshadowed both the Tabernacle and the Israelites in their desert journey. "The cloud of the Lord hovered over the Tabernacle by day, and there was fire in the cloud by night, and the Israelites could see it at every stage of their journey" (Ex. 40:34ff; Num. 10:34). The same expression is used in a prophecy of Isaiah concerning the purified Jerusalem: "Then over every building on Mount Zion and on all her places of assembly the Lord will create a cloud of smoke by day and a bright flame of fire by night; for glory shall be spread over all as a covering and a canopy" (Isa. 4:5). The verb "overshadow" is again used in the transfiguration stories of Mark, Matthew and Luke (Lk. 9:34 and parallels). What happened to Mary can be best understood in the light of these biblical passages. God was present with her in the same special way as with the people on the journey through the desert, with Jesus, Moses and Elijah on the mountain of the transfiguration and as God will be present in the new Jerusalem.

The biblical evocations concerning the coming of the Spirit put the annunciation to Mary in a similar wide framework of meaning. The words of Gabriel recall what happened when Samuel anointed David: "The spirit of the Lord came upon David and was with him from that day onwards" (1 Sam. 16:13). A similar expression is used in a prophecy which looks forward to the messianic time of peace and justice, when "a spirit from on high is lavished upon us" (Isa. 32:15ff). Again the same promise is made in the announcement of Pentecost (Acts 1:8). In Mary's case too there is that intimate presence of God who, by the power of the Spirit, initiates new epochs in the history of salvation. Through this Spirit the royal house of David was established which later became the prefiguration of the Messiah's reign. Through this same Spirit Mary becomes the instrument for the birth of the Messiah. The same Spirit again empowers the church at Pentecost. Finally, when this Spirit will be poured out on all the people of this earth, the long-expected time of universal justice and peace will come. Gabriel's announcement thus draws Mary into God's ever new initiatives in the history of salvation.

It may be that the promise of the Spirit and the overshadowing by God's power extend the horizon not only forward towards the goal of creation but also backward to its origin. The priestly creation story told how at first God's Spirit hovered over the dark, chaotic waters of the earth and how God's word transformed the chaos into created order. Perhaps Luke wanted us to discover also this: that with the coming birth of the Messiah a new creation begins.

The mystery of the conception of Jesus is treated with discretion in the New Testament. Neither Mark nor John reports anything about it. Luke and Matthew explicitly refer to it in their annunciation stories (Lk. 1:34–35; Mt. 1:18, 20, 23), but elsewhere in their Gospels, even elsewhere in their infancy narratives, nothing more is said about it.

Without any hesitation the evangelists called Jesus not only Son of God but also Joseph's or the carpenter's son. They also mentioned Jesus' brothers and sisters (for instance Mk 3:31f; 6:3f; Lk. 4:22; Jn 1:45; from the church fathers onwards these brothers and sisters were by many considered to be Jesus' cousins). Moreover, Jesus came from the family of David, and it was his father Joseph who belonged to David's house (Mt. 1:20;

Plate 11: *"Annunciation", painting by William Congdon, USA. 1960.*

Lk. 1:27; 2:4f), not his mother Mary. She is presented as a descendant from a priestly family (Lk. 1:5, 36). Only later apocryphal gospels describe her also as a descendant of David. The New Testament genealogies indicate the fact of Jesus' Davidic descent through Joseph, and at the same time refer in an indirect way to his extraordinary conception (Mt. 1:16; Lk. 3:23).

When Jesus' opponents accused him of being an illegitimate child—an accusation often used in anti-Christian polemics from the second century onwards—he did not say that God engendered him, but that God, his Father, "sent" him (Jn 8:41f).

The biblical affirmation about the virginal conception of Jesus appeared in fact relatively late in the early Christians' reflection about who Jesus was. Even then this mystery was taught only with great circumspection. The public proclamation emphasized first of all that God made Jesus his Son by raising him from the dead. This is what Paul preached in the synagogue of Antioch: "We are here to give you the good news that God, who made the promise to the fathers, has fulfilled it for their children by raising Jesus from the dead, as indeed it stands written, in the second Psalm: 'You are my Son; this day I have begotten you' " (Acts 13:32f). The promise formerly made to the Israelite king was thus in a figurative way applied to the risen Christ. The same is affirmed in one of the oldest Christian creeds which Paul quotes to the Christians in Rome about the gospel of God's Son: "On the human level he was born of David's stock, but on the level of the spirit—the Holy Spirit—he was declared Son of God by a mighty act in that he rose from the dead" (Rom. 1:3f).

Early Christian reflection did not stop here. In the light of several Old Testament promises and remembering the words of Jesus as well as special events in his life, new insights of faith were gained. Jesus' becoming the Son of God was now dated backwards from his resurrection and placed at the earlier events of his baptism, transfiguration and crucifixion. The evangelist Mark became the first to record this conviction of faith (Mk 1:11; 9:7; 15:39; compare above p. 13f). While according to Mark's testimony the disciples could not yet grasp this, Matthew reports that Peter explicitly confessed: "You are the Messiah, the Son of the living God" (compare Mt. 16:16 and 14:33 with Mk 8:29 and 6:51f).

Later, when the traditions of faith behind the introductory chapters of Matthew and Luke were formed, Jesus was recognized as God's Son even from his conception onwards. Thus a second dating backwards occurred after that from the resurrection to the baptism, this time from Jesus' baptism and public ministry to his birth, even to his conception. The promise of Psalm 2:7 was now literally applied to Jesus in the annunciations to Joseph (Mt. 1:20ff) and to Mary (Lk. 1:30ff).

A parallel theological reflection led to the affirmation that in Jesus we meet the Word and Wisdom of God who existed already from the beginning of creation. Some biblical creeds (Phil. 2:6; Col. 1:15), and especially the evangelist John (Jn 1:1; 8:58; 17:5), testify that long before his conception and birth, in fact before all things were created, Jesus was "with God", "sharing God's appearance" and thus being "the image of the invisible God".

Annunciation

In Mark's prologue it was a human messenger who prepared the way for the coming of the Messiah: John the baptist, presented as the returning prophet Elijah. In the infancy narratives of Matthew and Luke a heavenly messenger appears on the scene. Matthew simply speaks of an "angel of the Lord" who made himself known to Joseph in a dream (Mt. 1:20; 2:13, 19). In Luke's story the messenger presents himself with a name and a function: "I am Gabriel; I stand in attendance upon God, and I have been sent to speak to you and bring you this good news" (Lk. 1:19, 26ff).

Originally such "angels of the Lord" indicated God's visible presence with people. In ancient Old Testament stories it can be interchangeably God or his angel who speaks. This happens, for instance, in the conversation between the run-away slave-girl Hagar and the angel of the Lord who appears there (and for the first time in the Bible). The story also forms an interesting parallel to the annunciations of birth in the infancy narratives of Matthew and Luke:

The angel of the Lord found Hagar by a spring of water in the wilderness . . . and said to her, "Go back to your mistress and submit to her ill-treatment." The angel also said, "I will make your descendants too many to be counted." And the angel of the Lord said to her:
"You are with child and will bear a son.
You shall name him Ishmael,
because the Lord has heard of your ill-treatment.
He shall be a man like the wild ass,
his hand against every man
and every man's hand against him;
and he shall live at odds with all his kinsmen."
She called the Lord who was speaking to her by the name El-Roi, for she said, "Have I indeed seen God and still live after that vision?" (Gen. 16:7–13).

The Jews returning from the Babylonian exile experienced God as a far-away and silent Lord. Prophecy came to an end and therefore the role of angels became much more important. They were now seen as personal beings, often with their own names, coming from the transcendent, heavenly world to act as messengers and interpreters of visions. Especially in apocalyptic spirituality and literature (compare above p. 16), a whole set of beliefs about angels developed, rejected by the Sadducees but critically accepted by the Pharisees. The writers of the New Testament presuppose the existence of such

heavenly messengers. The angels appear especially in the childhood narratives and the testimonies about the resurrection.

The angel Gabriel is first mentioned in the Bible as the interpreter of Daniel's visions (Dan. 8:15ff; 9:21ff). In intertestamental writings this messenger fulfills manifold functions, and he often appears together with the militant Michael and the healing Raphael, all of them belonging to the highest rank of heavenly messengers, the archangels. When he appears to Zechariah the angel Gabriel simply states his credentials (he stands in attendance on God) and his mission (sent to announce good news). The accent lies wholly on God's messages to Zechariah and Mary.

As one compares these messages, one is struck by both a remarkable parallelism and progression: God's initiative through John the baptist anticipates and prepares for God's initiative through Jesus. Yet—as the following juxtaposition of the two messages shows—there is also a clear emphasis on the superiority of Jesus' over the baptist's ministry.

Luke 1:13–17	*Luke 1:28–35*
Zechariah	*Hail, Mary most favoured one,*
do not be afraid!	*do not be afraid!*
Your prayer was heard:	*The Lord is with you:*
Your wife Elisabeth	*You shall conceive*
will bear you a son.	*and bear a son.*
Name him John.	*Give him the name Jesus.*
He will be great	*He will be great,*
before the Lord.	*the 'Son of the Most High'.*
Never touching wine,	*On the throne of David,*
filled with the Spirit,	*conceived by the Spirit,*
forerunner like Elijah.	*king over Israel.*
He will prepare a people	*His reign*
fit for the Lord.	*shall never end.*

In the two messages of Gabriel, the announcement of Jesus' birth to Joseph (Mt. 1:20–21) and the message of the angel of the Lord to Hagar about Ishmael, we notice a common pattern. The same pattern can be observed in the announcements of the birth of Isaac and Samson (Gen. 17:1–19; 18:1–15; Judg. 13:2–23). Luke obviously used this typically biblical way of telling an annunciation story. Yet in the message of Gabriel to Mary an altogether new content appears.

In the annunciation painted by Paul Woelfel (Plate 12) all the typical elements of biblical annunciation stories are present.

First of all the angel of the Lord appears. According to the biblical testimony only cherubim, seraphim and others in the heavenly host are said to have wings. Angels in the strict sense of the term (*angeloi*) always take the form of ordinary human beings. In Jacob's dream they needed a ladder to go up and down between heaven and earth, and when Gabriel first visited Daniel he appeared as "one with the semblance of a man" (Dan. 8:15). In earliest Christian art angels are consequently portrayed as human messengers. Only from the 4th century onwards are they portrayed with wings. But it is the coming with the power of the Spirit and with a divine message which invests Gabriel with angelic authority, not the small wings.

Secondly there is sometimes the fear and always the astonishment of the addressee. In Woelfel's painting Mary sits with great dignity on an African chair, overwhelmed with wonder. With the gesture of her right hand she asks in amazement: "Me?"

Thirdly and most importantly comes the message. Woelfel has painted it in the form of a letter from God, so holy that Gabriel does not even dare to touch it.

Fourthly, in biblical annunciation stories, the response to the message is often in the form of an objection or a request for a sign. The Mary in Woelfel's painting neither objects nor asks for a sign. With her left hand she signifies her readiness to be God's instrument, the channel of divine grace and the Spirit's power.

Finally, according to the biblical pattern, a sign is given. Consciously or unconsciously Woelfel has also included this element in his painting: the burning desert soil is transformed into a green meadow with flowers. They are the signs of the new life for this earth which comes with the birth of the Messiah.

Gabriel's appearance and message to Zechariah and Mary shows the continuity of God's action in the ongoing history of salvation. The Old Testament indeed foreshadows the New, as the *Biblia pauperum* shows so clearly (compare above pp. 29ff).

What happened to Zechariah and Elisabeth recalls Old Testament parents, equally old and barren, who nevertheless received a child: Abraham and Sarah with their child Isaac; Elkanah and Hannah with their child Samuel who was also destined to become a Nazarite, touching no wine. John the baptist resembles Samson, the Nazarite who was mightily stirred by God's Spirit (Judg. 13:25), and what John is called to do is described in terms of the prophecies of Malachi (Mal. 3:1; 4:5–6).

Gabriel's message to Mary contains also many allusions to the Old Testament. The affirmation that "nothing said by God can be impossible" echoes the divine question posed to Abraham and Sarah (Lk. 1:37; Gen. 18:14). Yet Mary reacts quite differently from Sarah. Her response is more like that of Hannah (1 Sam. 1:18). Jesus' ministry is described with the use of terms from the basic messianic text in the Old Testament, Nathan's promise to king David (compare Lk. 1:32–33 with 2 Sam. 7:8–16).

All these allusions to the Old Testament must not let us overlook what is new and unprecedented in Gabriel's annunciation to Mary. Jesus is here called "Son of God" not only in the sense in which the Davidic Messiah was given this title. Nor will he be made Son of God by virtue of his resurrection as the earliest Christian confessions state, or by virtue of what happened during his baptism, as Mark testified. From his conception onwards Jesus *is* the Son of God.

There is no precedent for such an affirmation in the Hebrew Old Testament. Isaiah's prophecy concerning the Immanuel (Isa. 7:14) speaks about "a young woman who is (or will be) with child". The accent there lies on the child, not the way of his conception. The later Greek translation made of the young woman a "virgin" thus shifting the emphasis from the child to the mother. This Greek translation of Isaiah was used by the early church which re-read it in the light of New Testament faith and understood it as a prophecy of the virginal conception of the Messiah (Mt. 1:22f). Gabriel's message to Mary announces this extraordinary creative act which initiates a new period in God's history of salvation.

In Woelfel's painting a meaningful detail points to this new divine initiative. When Moses met the angel of the Lord in the flame of the burning bush he took off his sandals (Ex. 3:1–6). When Gabriel visits Mary, the one chosen to become the mother of the Son of God, it is he who takes off the sandals, and kneels barefooted as he conveys the message.

Plate 12: *"Annunciation", water-colour by Paul Woelfel, Nigeria. Contemporary.*

The poor are lifted up

Red, black, yellow and white are the colours of majesty in the western part of the Pacific island New Britain. Edward Meli, a Melanesian artist from that region of Papua-New Guinea, has used these colours together with other traditional symbolism to interpret what happened at the annunciation (Plate 13). The messenger of the majestic God addresses the lowly Mary, and by this act a transformation takes place: the girl from Nazareth, a village of Galilee which was never even mentioned in the Old Testament, is clothed with majesty. Taking up a hymn from the "poor of the Lord" she sings:

Tell out, my soul, the greatness of the Lord,
rejoice, rejoice, my spirit, in God my saviour;
so tenderly has he looked upon his servant,
humble as she is.
For, from this day forth,
all generations will count me blessed,
so wonderfully has he dealt with me,
the Lord, the Mighty One.
His name is Holy;
his mercy sure from generation to generation
towards those who fear him;
the deeds his own right arm has done
disclose his might:
the arrogant of heart and mind he has put to rout,
he has brought down monarchs from their thrones,
but the humble have been lifted high.
The hungry he has satisfied with good things,
the rich sent empty away.
He has ranged himself at the side of Israel his servant;
firm in his promise to our forefathers,
he has not forgotten to show mercy to Abraham
and his children's children, for ever (Lk. 1:46–55).

Mary is sometimes seen as an essentially submissive, "humble" woman, the stereotype of the "handmaid" against which many women rightly revolt today. Humble she was, but with that particular biblical humility which is the opposite of passive resignation.

The challenging song which Mary sang has many parallels in Old Testament prayers and psalms. They originate from the *anawim*, the "poor or humble of the Lord". It was Zephaniah, the lonely prophet of judgment, who first described this group of faithful in a word addressed by God to the inhabitants of Jerusalem:

Then I will rid you
of your proud and arrogant citizens,
and never again shall you flaunt your pride
on my holy hill.
But I will leave in you a people
afflicted and poor . . .
(They) shall find refuge
in the name of the Lord (Zeph. 3:11ff).

These *anawim* did not passively accept their material and spiritual poverty. In prayer they struggled with the God who seemed to have abandoned them, challenging him to come and bring rescue. Their humility was thus not primarily a state of mind but a factual state of powerlessness, oppression and lowliness. In that situation, instead of turning their backs to God in bitter resignation, they cried out of their depths:

My God, my God, why have you forsaken me
and are so far from saving me,
from heeding my groans? (Ps. 22:1).

Out of the depths have I called
to you, O Lord;
Lord, hear my cry! (Ps. 130:1).

While those who first prayed in such words remain unknown, the suffering prophet Jeremiah and Job in their deep distress are well-known exponents of this spirituality of God's *anawim*. What characterizes them is their struggle with God in prayer that he may manifest himself and that his cause may ultimately win. Like great gamblers, they take the risk of putting their whole stake on that God who often seems so far away—and in the truth of God's promises. With a hope against all human hopes they cling to the assurance that ultimately God's plan of salvation will be realized.

Mary was one among such *anawim*. In Meli's painting she appears with a total concentration, ready to accept God's purpose for her as announced by Gabriel. The colours and graphic design with which she is painted integrate her fully into the overall pattern. From now on her identity can no longer be separated from the message she receives. Therefore she responds:

Here am I,
I am the Lord's servant;
as you have spoken,
so be it! (Lk. 1:38).

Mary has two predecessors in the history of the people of Israel. One is well-known and often mentioned: Hannah, the mother of Samuel. The other is a strange, militant woman and seldom associated with Mary: Judith, whose exploits are recorded in an inter-testamental book which is named after her.

Plate 13: "Annunciation", panel painted by Edward Meli, West New Britain, Papua-New Guinea. Contemporary.

Hannah, humiliated because she was childless, continued year after year her struggle of prayer. Like others from among God's poor, the *anawim*, she poured out her heart before the Lord and made the vow that if she should receive a boy, he would for his whole life be devoted to the service of God (1 Sam. 1). Her request for a boy was granted, and when she brought him to the temple in Siloh she sang her mighty Magnificat, not as "humble" as many Christians would like to have it:

My heart rejoices in the Lord,
in the Lord I now hold my head high,
my mouth is full of derision of my foes,
exultant because you have saved me.
There is none except you,
none so holy as the Lord,
no rock like our God.
Cease your proud boasting,
let no word of arrogance pass your lips;
for the Lord is a God of all knowledge . . .
The Lord kills and he gives life,
he sends down to Sheol,
he can bring the dead up again . . .
He lifts the weak out of the dust
and raises the poor from the dunghill;
to give them a place among the great,
to set them in seats of honour . . .
Those that stand against the Lord will be terrified
when the High God thunders out of heaven.
The Lord is judge even to the ends of the earth,
he will give strength to his king
and raise high the head of his annointed prince.
(1 Sam. 2:1–10)

Judith's was a different kind of struggle. She lived in a situation of crisis, when the great general Holophernes was leading up his army from the East to wipe out the Israelites. Judith then turned to God with a typical prayer of the *anawim*: "Your might lies not in numbers nor your sovereign power in strong men; but you are the God of the humble, the help of the poor, the support of the weak, the protector of the desperate, the deliverer of the hopeless" (Judith 9:11). Then with grim courage she went to the enemy and used her womanly charm to deceive him. Filled with an ardent longing to possess her, Holophernes "drank a great deal of wine, more indeed, than he had ever drunk". And this was the moment for Judith. Singlehandedly she decapitated the mighty Holophernes with his own sword. When she returned, the magistrate of her city welcomed her with words similar to those Gabriel addressed Mary.

The blessing of God Most High is upon you,
you more than all other women on earth!

And Judith responded with a canticle of praise which, like Hannah's song, in many ways anticipates Mary's Magnificat (Judith 13:18; 16:1ff).

Representing all the *anawim*, Mary also offers herself, body and soul, to be totally available for God's purpose:

As you have spoken, so be it.

By thus totally submitting to the Lord's will she becomes the first disciple of the one she conceives. Luke indeed portrays Mary as the model of Christian discipleship. That discipleship leads to a "high revolt", yet a revolt quite different from that of Judith. The struggle is not just for the protection of one nation but for the salvation of all peoples on this earth. Evil cannot be overcome by slaughter and hatred, but by love of the enemy and costly forgiveness, as Jesus later taught. The vicious circle of repression and rebellion must not be continued, with more and yet more violence inflicted on others. It is to be broken only by an act of self-sacrifice. This is the "high revolt" sung by Mary, and only with *this* understanding may we join in Mary's song as Fred Kaan has transcribed it for today:

Sing we a song of high revolt;
make great the Lord, his name exalt!
Sing we the song that Mary sang,
of God at war with human wrong.

Sing we of him who deeply cares
and still with us our burden bears.
He who with strength the proud disowns,
brings down the mighty from their thrones.

By him the poor are lifted up;
he satisfies with bread and cup
the hungry men of many lands;
the rich must go with empty hands.

He calls us to revolt and fight
with him for what is just and right,
to sing and live "Magnificat"
in crowded street and council flat.

The Saviour of the world

"He was sent as a Saviour, for us and for those who come after us, one who should cause wars to cease, and should set all things in fair order. When he came the hopes of those who looked forward to a better future were made to appear poor compared with the reality . . ." Thus "good news went forth into the world since the birthday of God".

One would expect to find the above quotation in Luke's Gospel or some other early Christian writing. It was in fact a message issued several years before the birth of Jesus by a Roman proconsul, hewn in stone as an announcement to the people in Asia Minor. It refers to the great Roman Caesar Augustus who reigned from 31 B.C. to A.D. 14. After many decades of war he indeed brought peace to the Roman empire. In Rome the temple of the war-god Janus, whose doors stood open during times of fighting, could finally be closed. Instead an altar to the "Peace of Augustus" was being built.

It was this famous Augustus who—according to Luke—became a servant for God's plan of salvation. More than five hundred years earlier, the mighty Persian conqueror Cyrus had been used in a similar way. His decree of 538 B.C. brought to an end the Babylonian exile and brought at least part of the people of Israel back to Palestine. The great prophet of the exile, commonly called the Second Isaiah, welcomed Cyrus as God's anointed one, as a Messiah (Isa. 45:1ff; text of Cyrus' decree in Ezra 1:2–4). Now a decree from the world ruler Augustus brought Joseph and Mary to Bethlehem, where the true deliverer, *the* Messiah and Lord, would be born: "In those days a decree was issued by the Emperor Augustus for a registration to be made throughout the Roman world. This was the first registration of its kind; it took place when Quirinius was governor of Syria. For this purpose everyone made his way to his own town; and so Joseph went up to Judaea from the town of Nazareth in Galilee, to register at the city of David, called Bethlehem, because he was of the house of David by descent; and with him went Mary who was betrothed to him" (Lk. 2:1–5).

As a matter of fact, the census conducted under Quirinius covered only Judaea, not Galilee, and it happened at least 10 years after Jesus' birth (in A.D. 6/7, while Jesus was born before Herod's death, thus at the latest in 4 B.C.). Also elsewhere in Luke's two-volume Gospel there are similar inaccuracies in dating events. The mention of Augustus, and also perhaps of the census, has theological significance: it indicates that Caesar's peace, the *pax Augusta*, is being surpassed by God's peace, the *pax Christi*. Maybe Luke also wanted attentive readers to recall another census in the history of the people of Israel, that of king David (2 Sam. 24). It brought the disaster of pestilence upon the people. This new census, however, will bring the good news and great joy to the inhabitants of the earth.

The theological meaning of Luke's story is well expressed in the Eastern Orthodox icon of the nativity whose main features had been fixed from the tenth century onwards. Iconographers do not set out to represent historic events and earthly realities from a human point of view. Rather, they portray the here and now already in its process of transfiguration. They look at people and things from God's point of view. Time is taken up into eternity, so that on the icon subsequent events can be painted together, for instance Jesus lying in the crib, and Jesus being bathed.

Icons do not illustrate a biblical story, but they visually express the Christian faith. They are painted creeds and prayers. For many centuries theologians, bishops and lay people passionately discussed whether such pictorial representations are theologically legitimate. In the Eastern Orthodox Church the decisive argument for the icon was accepted at the seventh ecumenical council of Nicea, A.D. 787: "The making of pictorial representations corresponds to the history of the preaching of the gospel. It is a tradition useful in many respects, but especially for showing that the incarnation of the Word of God is real and not just imaginary."

While the icon of the transfiguration gives us a key for the right meditation on all icons, the icon of nativity points to the basic theological justification of all Christian art, namely the incarnation of God's Word.

Luke's narration of the event connected with the birth of Jesus provides the basic elements for the icon of nativity (compare the late 16th century version of this icon, reproduced on plate 14). From Luke 2:1–20 iconographers received the images of the newborn child, wrapped in swaddling bands and lying in the manger; Mary resting beside the child, with Joseph sitting close by; an angel announcing the good news to a shepherd and other angels singing "Glory to God".

Other features were added in order to emphasize the dogma of the incarnation: the good news is not only for the shepherds who represent the people of Israel, but also for the Gentiles. Therefore *the journey of the Magi* was included from Matthew's Gospel. The incarnation has significance even for the animal world. Already from the 4th century onwards *the ox and the donkey* form an integral part of the nativity scene (especially in

Russian icons, a horse often replaces the donkey). The animals show that Isaiah's prophecy has been fulfilled: "The ox knows its owner and the ass its master's stall" (Isa. 1:3). In a later apocryphal infancy gospel ("Pseudo Matthew" from the 8th/9th century) this prophecy was understood as pointing to the adoration of Christ by the whole universe: "Thus the beasts, ox and ass, with him (Christ) between them, unceasingly worshipped him."

From the 7th century onwards the scene with a midwife and her helper *bathing the newborn child* was introduced into the nativity icon. It comes from the 2nd century apocryphal infancy gospel of James, where not the actual bath but the presence of a midwife is mentioned. This legendary scene became dogmatically important because it emphasizes that Jesus not only appeared to be human, but was actually born as a human child and needed a bath like any newly born infant. Also the *cave as birth place* is mentioned in the infancy gospel of James, but it may go back to an oral tradition from Bethlehem. The first church in Bethlehem, erected at the request of Helena, the mother of emperor Constantine, was indeed built above a cave.

The *star* is taken from Matthew's account, and soon received various shades of meaning, based on the prophecy by Balaam (Num. 24:17) and passages in the book of Isaiah (Isa. 9:2; 60:1–3). Part of the circle of heaven appears on the icon from which the star with its light cuts open the mountain and the cave. Through colour symbolism a link is established between Jesus' nativity and his transfiguration.

The *person with the staff* speaking with the thoughtful Joseph has been variously interpreted. Is it the prophet Isaiah? Or does it portray the devil who tempts Joseph not to believe in the miracle of the virginal conception? Probably neither of these understandings is the right one. Traditional iconographic representations of both Isaiah and the devil differ considerably from the one who addresses Joseph. Presumably the figure merely represents an old shepherd.

Meditating on this icon of the nativity, the Orthodox Church recites during the vespers of Christmas Day the prayer of Patriarch Germanos of the 8th century:

What can we offer to you, O Christ,
you who came for our sake on earth as a human being?
Each creature exists through you and gives you thanks:
the angels their song, the heavens the star,
the Magi their gifts, the shepherds their miracle,
the earth the cave, the desert the manger,
and we a virgin mother.
O God who is before all time,
have mercy on us.

Plate 14: *Icon of nativity, Greek icon. Ca. 1580.*

Be welcome, my God, my Lord, my Son

The earliest nativity scenes of Christian art portray only the child in the manger with the ox and the donkey. When later Mary appears, she sits, or lies down, tired and uninvolved, near the manger, often turning her head away from the child. In the Christmas scene of Plate 15, however, we see a very healthy Mary kneeling and adoring the just-born child. The boy needs no bath, nor is he clothed in swaddling bands. The manger is empty. In the corner old Joseph absent-mindedly cooks some food. This presentation of the birth forms the central New Testament image on the page devoted to the nativity in the Heidelberg manuscript of the *Biblia pauperum* (compare above pp. 29ff).

Compared with the classic icon of the nativity (Plate 14) there is here a new perception of what happened at Bethlehem. The four prophets and the two Old Testament scenes which appear on the same page of the *Biblia pauperum* are not reproduced here. Both Old Testament types point to Mary's virginity. The first episode which foreshadows Jesus' birth is the burning bush from which God spoke to Moses (Ex. 3). The accompanying text explains that just as the fire burns but does not consume the green leaves, so Mary gave birth but still maintained her virginity as before, during and after delivery. The second Old Testament scene shows the priest Aaron whose staff alone blossomed and brought forth almonds in the tabernacles (Num. 17). Again typological interpretation sees in this sign a pointer to the extraordinary birth of Jesus and to Mary's virginity.

To many Christians in the 20th century such typological correspondences between the Old and the New Testaments may sound arbitrary and far-fetched. The church fathers had already pointed to these correspondences. Theodoret of Cyrus (†458) says to those who do not understand such symbolism: "Do you not know that the events of the Old Covenant fore-shadow the New Covenant? For our mysteries (of faith) are portrayed already in the old images . . . Do you not recognize the virgin in the burning bush?" The correspondence between the blossoming staff of Aaron and virgin Mary giving birth to Jesus was familiar to medieval spirituality. The first verse of the then very popular Melker song on Mary, written around 1135, tells:

Once did Aaron
put on earth a branch.
It gave birth to almonds,
nuts so wonderful:
This sweetness you brought forth,
Mother without help of man,
Sancta Maria.

To the right of Mary is seen an ancient biblical symbol: a stump out of which springs a blossoming new shoot. It clearly recalls Isaiah's prophecy that "a shoot shall grow from the stock of Jesse . . .", a text which played an important role in the messianic expectations (Isa. 11:1–5; compare above pp. 13ff). On the whole, however, this page of the *Biblia pauperum* reflects a type of medieval piety centred on Mary more than Luke's testimony to Jesus' birth, like the page of the same manuscript examined earlier dealing with the Annunciation.

With many variations the new perception of what happened in Bethlehem has continued to be reflected in Western art. The origin of this perception lies in a vision of St Birgitta of Sweden.

Birgitta of Sweden was a most remarkable woman. Born at the beginning of the turbulent 14th century (1302), she spent the first half of her life thoroughly involved in human and political affairs. Her parents were closely related to the Swedish royal family; she was the wife of a prince, and the mother of eight children; and she was influential in the Swedish court. After the death of her husband and in response to a vision she founded in 1346 a religious order for the reform of the church's life. The order soon spread all over Europe. It was originally conceived as a joint community of monks and nuns. Birgitta continued to play an important role in European church and state affairs, but increasingly her attention was directed towards Palestine.

Even before the death of her husband, Mary had promised Birgitta in a vision that she would see Christ—how he was born in Bethlehem and how he died on the cross. In a later vision she received from Mary the following summons: "You shall come to the Holy City, when it pleases my son. From there you shall come to Bethlehem, where I will show you in every particular how it happened, when I gave birth to my son there."

A year before her death in 1371 Birgitta received the summons. Immediately she left on a pilgrimage to

Plate 15: *Nativity. New Testament central image of page on the nativity in* Biblia pauperum, *Heidelberg Manuscript. First half 15th century.*

Palestine. There she had visions at the major stations of Jesus' life. These she wrote down in her *Revelationes*, a manuscript which had wide circulation in Europe. Especially after the canonization of Birgitta as a saint in 1391, her revelations had a great influence on Western religious art.

This is the vision Birgitta received when praying in the grotto of the nativity at Bethlehem: "I saw a Virgin of extreme beauty wrapped in a white mantle and a delicate tunic through which I perceived her virgin body soon to be delivered. With her was an old man of great honesty, and they brought with them an ox and a donkey. They entered the cave, and having tied the animals to the manger, the man went outside and brought to the virgin a burning candle. After attaching this to the wall he went outside so that he might not be present at the birth.

"Then the virgin pulled off her shoes from her feet, drew the white mantle that enveloped her, removed the veil from her head, laying it by her side, thus remaining in her tunic only with her beautiful golden hair falling loosely down her shoulders . . . Then the virgin, kneeling with great reverence, placed herself in prayer, with her back to the crib, her face eastward, raised to heaven. She stood with uplifted hands, her eyes fixed on heaven, rapt, as it were, in an ecstasy of contemplation, in a rapture of divine sweetness. And while she stood in prayer, I saw her child move in her womb and at once, in a twinkling of an eye, she brought forth her son, from whom such ineffable light and splendour radiated that the sun could not be compared to it.

"So sudden and momentary was that mode of bearing that I could not perceive or discern how, or in what part she brought forth. Nevertheless, I immediately beheld that glorious babe lying naked and most pure on the ground, his flesh most clean from any kind of soil or impurity. Then I heard angelic chants of wonderful sweetness. When the virgin felt that she already had born her child, she immediately worshipped him, her head bent down and her hands clasped, with great reverence, and said to him: 'Be welcome my God, my Lord, my Son!' "

What they had heard and seen

Shortly before the lonely Rembrandt died in 1669, he was working on his last painting: old Simeon holding Jesus in his arms as if the infant were the most precious treasure. During the first part of his life the Dutch painter used to admire quite other treasures. He had been a passionate collector of costly and beautiful artefacts. But the inventory of his possessions made after his death lists only a few items. Among them just one book, the Bible.

For the young and successful Rembrandt the Bible had simply been a quarry from which he took dramatic subjects for his art. Then, after the death of three of his children, of his mother, and, in 1642, of his beloved wife Saskia, and when his particular style of painting met with less and less public appreciation, the biblical message began to penetrate both the artist and his work. More than two centuries later another great Dutch artist, Vincent van Gogh, summed this up in just one sentence: "There is Rembrandt in the Gospel and the Gospel in Rembrandt."

One of the passages of the gospel story to which Rembrandt came back again and again was the narrative about the birth of Jesus (Lk. 2:1–20). Before looking at this scene through the eyes of the Dutch painter it is important to see how the "painter" Luke portrays what the shepherds had heard and seen.

When at night they are in the field, suddenly an angel of the Lord stands before them "and the splendour of the Lord shone round them". As soon as they hear the good news the shepherds say to one another: "Come, we must go straight to Bethlehem and see this thing that has happened."

What they actually find is nothing extraordinary: no palace, no golden background, no throne for Mary, no gifts from royal visitors. Even the angels are not there. The shepherds meet only two ordinary people, travellers in a temporary shelter, and a new-born baby. As in Matthew's Gospel, in Luke's account too the actual birth of the child is mentioned with a minimum of words, in the original Greek with no more than half a sentence (Mt. 2:1; Lk. 2:7). Nor is the place of birth clearly described.

The word usually translated as "the inn" occurs once more in Luke's Gospel, designating the room in which the Lord's supper took place (Lk. 2:7; 22:11; a different term is used for the innkeeper's house in the parable on the Good Samaritan). Luke gives us to understand that there was no more place in the common room for guests at an ordinary house or a caravanserai, but that Joseph and Mary found shelter in the adjacent barn.

It is striking that within ten verses the manger is mentioned three times and the swaddling clothes twice. Such very ordinary things become the sign given to the shepherds by the angel. Swaddling clothes do not suggest poverty. Solomon, the richest king in Israel's history, says in an inter-testamental book about himself: "When I was born, . . . I was carefully swaddled and nursed. No king begins life in any other way" (Wisd. 7:3ff). By and large, no emphasis is put on the poverty of the place or on the heartlessness of a supposed innkeeper. It is the manger and the response of the shepherds that are highlighted. Probably Luke wants to remind us of Isaiah's complaint, where also in the Greek translation the term manger occurs: "The ox knows its owner and the donkey knows the manger of its lord; but Israel, my own people, has no knowledge, no discernment" (Isa. 1:3).

Indeed from the very beginning of Christian art the ox and the donkey have appeared in nativity scenes, but Luke's account reminds us of the second half of Isaiah's complaint: good news has been proclaimed to God's own people, and now—unlike in the time of Isaiah—the Israelite shepherds did have discernment. They heard of the birth, and went to see the child in the manger. Moreover, "they recounted what they had been told about this child; and all who heard were astonished at what the shepherds said". Then they "returned glorifying and praising God for what they had heard and seen" (Lk. 2:16–18, 20).

The Adoration of the Shepherds (Plate 16) was painted in 1646, five years before Rembrandt's death. By now the biblical message had penetrated the artist and his work. In fact, the painter simply attempts to hear and see and communicate for his own time what the shepherds heard and saw.

The shepherds have just rushed into the barn: a boy holding a dog, a woman with a child in her arms, a few men and two other women, with a girl struck with wonder in between them, all ordinary people. Some continue to talk, but those who have seen Jesus in the manger have suddenly become silent. Mary sits near her first-born, surrounding him with care, and Joseph stands behind them. The splendour of God shines no more from above around the shepherds. Only the newborn child is lit up by a lamp behind the kneeling man, and the human faces reflect the light of this and other oil-lamps.

At first sight nothing extraordinary seems to happen in this scene from rural life. Yet as one meditates upon the predominantly dark and brown painting, one is overcome with the same awe which the persons around the infant Jesus express with different gestures.

What W. A. Visser 't Hooft wrote about the way in which Rembrandt painted the Christmas event is indeed true: "Among the great artists Rembrandt is one of the few who in their representation of the Christmas story have expressed the whole paradoxical harshness of the Incarnation. The great majority of painters do not allow the gospel to speak for itself, but make of the Christmas story either a poetic legend acted in celestial spheres, or else quite a worldly event. Few of them have grasped the importance of accepting the mystery of the birth of God's Son without giving it a purely divine or purely earthly interpretation."

The shepherds "returned glorifying and praising God for what they had heard and seen". As yet no discordant note is heard in the song of the angels and the adoration offered by ordinary people. True, not all have joined in it: the priests and Pharisees and other especially pious people are not there. To persons without a name, to shepherds who in Jesus' time had a low social status, the news of what had happened was addressed. They were the first to make the awesome discovery of the Messiah.

When later Joseph and Mary went to the temple in Jerusalem and, according to the Jewish law, presented their first-born to God, the first discordant note in the harmony of praise was heard. It was sounded by Simeon, a man "upright and devout, one who watched and waited for the restoration of Israel" (Lk. 2:25). At first he too joined in the praise with his famous "Nunc Dimittis". Then, still holding the child Jesus in his arms, Simeon blessed the parents and said to Mary: "This child is destined to be a sign which people reject; and you too shall be pierced to the heart. Many in Israel will stand or fall because of him, and thus the secret thoughts of many will be laid bare" (Lk. 2:34f).

Rembrandt, like Simeon, knew what follows after the glorious overture of Luke's infancy narratives. He therefore became the painter of the cross. And when shortly before his death he worked on his last painting— Simeon with Jesus in his arms—he must have deeply meditated not only on what the shepherds heard and saw, but also on what Simeon perceived.

Plate 16: *Adoration of the Shepherds, painting by Rembrandt, Netherlands. 1646.*

In the city of David

"So Joseph went up to Judaea from the town of Nazareth in Galilee, to register in the city of David, called—Bethlehem." Those familiar with the Old Testament would have expected a journey to Jerusalem. For Jerusalem is normally called the "city of David" and "to go up to" is both in the Old and the New Testament the standard expression for ascending to Jerusalem.

There is in Luke's Gospel a strange dialectical relationship between Jerusalem with its temple and the oikoumene beyond Jerusalem. On the one hand the infancy stories begin with the priest Zechariah in the temple. Then, at the time prescribed by the Jewish Law, Jesus is brought up to Jerusalem so that he may be consecrated to the Lord. Finally, Luke's infancy narratives conclude with the scene of the twelve-year-old boy Jesus "sitting in the temple surrounded by the teachers, listening to them and putting questions". Yet, on the other hand, the key events of the story happen outside of Jerusalem: the angel Gabriel announces the birth of Jesus to Mary in Galilee, the birth itself occurs in Bethlehem, and the first proclamation of the good news with the subsequent human response of praise—the first Christian worship, so to say—happens among common shepherd people outside in the field.

As was shown when introducing the evangelist Luke (above pp. 26ff) this is a characteristic feature not only of the infancy narratives but of the whole two-volume Gospel of Luke. The good news about Christ the Lord is intimately interwoven with the history and expectations of the people of Israel; yet the message concerns the Saviour of the *world*, to be announced to the Gentiles. All human actors on the Palestinian scene in Luke's infancy narratives are Jews. Yet it is the Roman emperor who set the stage, and the good news proclaimed to the shepherds will spread, beyond every frontier of race and language and continent, to the ends of the earth.

Thus, in the 16th and 17th centuries Luke's account of Jesus' birth also reached the Muslim rulers in North India. They must have particularly liked this story, for many of the miniatures painted by Muslim and Hindu artists at the Mogul courts show Mary and the birth of Christ. The earliest of these miniatures are simply copies of European Christian art. Later, more genuinely Indian interpretations were created, such as the one reproduced on Plate 17. It must have been a Hindu artist who painted it, because both Mary and Joseph carry the sign of their Hindu caste on their forehead. The persons adoring the child were freely chosen from the gospel stories, presumably portraying the devout Simeon, the prophetess Anna and behind Mary the apostle John.

The Mogul rulers knew about Mary and Jesus long before the Gospel stories were interpreted to them through Christian art. In their own Holy Scripture, the Koran, they could read about Mary and the circumstances under which she gave birth to Jesus whom the Muslims call the prophet Isa. Mary is the only woman called by her proper name in the Koran and she is there mentioned no less than thirty-four times, more often than in the New Testament.

The Koran tells about the annunciation of the virginal conception of Jesus (compare Sura 19:22ff which has many parallels with Lk. 1:26ff). It includes a description of Jesus' birth, which has been influenced by later Christian apocryphal childhood gospels: Mary gives birth to Jesus under a palm-tree and makes a fast. When she takes the child back to her people she is accused of adultery: "Mary pointed to the child then; but they said: 'How shall we speak to one who is still in the cradle, a little child?' He (Jesus) said, 'Lo, I am God's servant; God has given me the Book, and made me a Prophet; Blessed He has made me, wherever I may be; and He has enjoined me to pray, and to give the alms, so long as I live, and likewise to cherish my mother.' . . . 'Surely God is my Lord, and your Lord; so serve you Him. This is a straight path' " (Sura 19:30ff).

This miracle child of the Koran is obviously not the Jesus of the New Testament. Have Christian art and its Hindu-Muslim adaptations led the Mogul rulers to a fuller understanding of Jesus? We do not know. Yet who could ever claim to know in all its fullness the mind and love of him who was born in Bethlehem? As the gospel of his birth, death and resurrection reaches people of other faiths, cultures and ages, ever new aspects of the Immanuel will be discovered.

"Today in the city of David a deliverer has been born to you—the Messiah, the Lord" (Lk. 2:11). This announcement by the angel of the Lord to the shepherds in the field also did not refer to Jerusalem, *the* city of David, but to Bethlehem. The shepherds understood this. They immediately say to one another: "Come, we must go straight to *Bethlehem*" (Lk. 2:15).

For those living in the biblical oral traditions, thinking thus by association more than by logical reasoning,

Plate 17: *The Holy Family with three persons adoring the child. Painting by an unknown (Hindu?) artist for the Muslim Mogul kings. India. First half of the 17th century.*

the reference to shepherds indeed evokes Bethlehem more than Jerusalem. Did not David, the shepherd, come from that village? In the fields around, the future great shepherd–ruler over Judah and Israel had kept watch over his father's flock. There on God's command, the prophet Samuel had singled out the youngest among Jesse's sons, the boy David, who had first to be fetched from the fields: "This is the man!" And "Samuel took the horn of oil and anointed him in the presence of his brothers. Then the spirit of the Lord came upon David and was with him from that day onwards" (1 Sam. 16:11ff).

Among the many confused expectations in Jesus' time about the coming of the Messiah were also echoes of old prophecies like this: "Does not Scripture say that the Messiah is to be of the family of David, from David's village of Bethlehem?" (Jn 7:42). As Matthew's story about the Magi shows, the Scripture referred to was the oracle of Micah about Bethlehem (Mic. 5:2; Mt. 2:4f).

In the fourth and fifth chapters of Micah there is a correlation between Jerusalem/Zion and Bethlehem, similar to the one we find in Luke's infancy narratives:

Micah 4–5	*Luke 2*
Jerusalem is humiliated by Babylonian armies (4:10–11)	*Palestine is incorporated into the Roman empire (2:1–5)*
Yet the enemies do not know God's thought (4:12)	*Yet God takes a new initiative (2:9ff)*
All the nations will come streaming to Jerusalem to be taught God's ways (4:1–2)	*The census moves the nations; good news is proclaimed to Israel and the Gentiles (2:1ff, 10, 32)*
There will be universal peace (4:3ff)	*Peace on earth is now announced (2:14)*
It will be like a woman in labour (4:10; 5:3)	*A woman gives birth to a son (2:7, 11f)*
The liberator comes not from Jerusalem, but from Bethlehem (5:2ff)	*Not in Jerusalem, but in Bethlehem the Messiah is found (2:10ff)*

Micah's description of the liberator is strikingly similar to Luke's account of the ministry of Jesus before and after his ascension:

He shall appear and be their shepherd
in the strength of the Lord,
in the majesty of the name of the Lord his God.
And they (his family) shall continue,
for now his greatness shall reach
to the ends of the earth;
and he shall be a man of peace (Mic. 5:4f).

Yet—one may well ask, in the light of recent events in this part of the world—has this peace from Bethlehem really reached the region from which it came? Have not the populations of Palestine and the whole of the surrounding region met hatred and death instead of Christ's love and life?

Gloria in excelsis

There is much singing in the infancy narratives of Luke's Gospel. Immediately after the angel of the Lord had announced the good news there appeared "a great company of the heavenly host, singing the praises of God:

Glory to God in the highest heaven,
and on earth peace among people of (his) favour.

The second part of this song of glory can be differently translated. If the term "favour" stands in the genitive case ("people of favour", as the oldest and best Greek manuscripts read), the song is the two-line canticle rendered above. If, however, the term "favour" stands in the nominative case (as it appears in some old manuscripts), we have a three-line canticle:

Glory to God in the highest heaven,
and on earth peace,
(and) among people (God's) favour!

Whatever version one follows, it is important to note that *God*'s glory, peace and favour are sung. Peace is given to people whom God favours. Who are these favoured ones? Luke uses the term only two more times in his Gospel. First during the baptism of Jesus, when a voice from heaven acknowledged him: "You are my Son, my Beloved; on you my favour rests" (Lk. 3:22). The term occurs a second time when Jesus comforted his disciples who were about to face persecution: "Have no fear, little flock; for it is the favour of your Father to give you the kingdom" (Lk. 12:32). In the Gospels the kingdom is promised in this outspoken way only to children, to the poor and to those who are persecuted for the cause of right. Mary sang in her Magnificat about the God who favours and uplifts the poor (compare above pp. 38ff). Now the heavenly hosts announce this same God to the shepherds.

The angelic appearance and hymn recall the moment when the prophet Isaiah experienced a theophany, a manifestation of God in the temple of Jerusalem. He saw the Lord seated on a throne, and about him the attendant seraphim. "They were calling ceaselessly to one another:

Holy, holy, holy is the Lord of Hosts:
the whole earth is full of his glory (Isa. 6:3).

In Jewish literature of the time of Jesus, when the heavenly hosts see how God is doing something new and decisive in creation and history, they often respond in songs of praise. The angel of the Lord announces the decisive "today" of the deliverer's birth (Lk. 2:11), and immediately heaven resounds with songs of glory.

It elicits an echo of praise on earth. When the shepherds had seen God's favoured peace-maker in the person of a vulnerable infant they respond to the hymn from heaven with their own song. They "returned glorifying and praising God for what they had heard and seen".

Since then the human response with songs of praise has never ceased. In his two-volume Gospel Luke again and again dwells on the response, with joy and songs, of the church to God's action in history. Only Luke reports that when Jesus entered Jerusalem, the "Peace on earth" sung by the heavenly host at Jesus' birth is answered with a parallel hymn sung by the multitude of disciples:

In heaven peace,
and glory in the highest heaven! (Lk. 19:38).

The angel with the trumpet, atop the bamboo crib, accompanies a whole choir of singing angels. In the present reproduction of this crib from Taiwan (Plate 18) only three musicians and two candle-bearers could be shown, but the original crib includes a great company of the heavenly host who sing a mighty song.

This song of praise on the fields near Bethlehem during that first Christmas night has found many echoes down the centuries and in all continents: poems, hymns, religious plays and oratorios centre mainly on Luke's infancy narratives. Today Christmas carols and nativity plays are the most popular among Christian songs and dramas all over the world. This has not always been the case.

The early church sang and celebrated the victory of Christ's cross and resurrection long before Christmas hymns and liturgies were composed. Even as the narratives of the nativity were probably written after the church had confessed Jesus as the crucified and risen Lord, the liturgical celebration of the birth of Christ started relatively late; among the majority of Christians it began only from the 4th century onwards. Actual nativity plays developed much later.

In the Eastern church a cycle of hymns written by the Patriarch Sophronius of Jerusalem (around 635) together form a first short nativity play. In the Western church liturgical plays about the shepherds appeared from the 11th century. They were patterned after the already existing Easter plays. In the course of the next few centuries, new scenes were added to the shepherds' play. A manuscript with text and music from the 13th century includes a nativity play which starts with the prophets testifying to the coming Messiah; it is followed by the disputation between the Ecclesia and the Synagogue, and leads to the annunciation to Mary, the scenes with the shepherds and of Herod with the Magi, of the murder of the infants, ending with the scene of the flight to Egypt.

Originally these were Latin plays, sung and enacted in the church buildings before or after the Christmas liturgy, as well as on special days of the Christmas season. From about 1200 onwards such plays appeared also in the people's languages, and three centuries later they moved out of the cathedrals to the market-place. Another development from the medieval nativity dramas was the later oratorios, among them such famous ones as the Christmas oratorios of Heinrich Schütz (1664) and Johann Sebastian Bach (1734). These are great artistic creations; they did not by any means halt the output of popular creativity, and ever new Christmas carols and nativity plays continue to be produced.

Meanwhile a new element of Christmas celebrations in the church and in homes became increasingly popular: the crib. It goes back to Francis of Assisi who decorated a crib at Greccio in 1223. Such Christmas cribs have since been fashioned by the hands of children and artists, in many cultures and centuries, for true devotion—and for the Christmas trade. Cribs are made of clay and stones, wood and metal, straw and cloth or still other fabrics as in the bamboo crib from Taiwan.

These can be a powerful help for remembering the story and meditating on its meaning, but Christmas cribs have in many ways also blurred the specific testimony of the evangelists. They usually incorporate part of Matthew's teaching into the story of Luke, and almost totally disregard the testimony of Mark and the vision of John. Even Luke's story is one-sidedly perceived, as when the crib emphasizes the poverty of Jesus' birth and evokes pity rather than joy. Luke's original testimony leads to songs of glory, because the great shepherd-king, the new David, the deliverer has now come.

This original message is well expressed in the words of D. T. Niles from Sri Lanka to the tune of a Korean carol:

On a day, when men were counted,
God became the Son of Man;
That his name, in every census,
Should be entered was his plan.
God, the Lord of all Creation,
Humbly takes a creature's place;
He, whose form no man has witnessed,
Has today a human face.

The carol ends with the words:

Out of Egypt came the Saviour
Man's Immanuel to be,—
Christmas shines with Easter glory,
Glory of eternity.

Plate 18: *Christmas crib. Made with bamboo; Potzu, Taiwan. Contemporary.*

But Mary pondered all these things

The shepherds have already left. They are back with their flock in the fields. The child is there, with Mary and Joseph: with them are three angels and a few remaining animals. Other messengers and creatures from the African steppe and jungle form part of this remarkable crib, sculptured by Alfred Mlangeni (Plate 19). They had joined in the praise of the whole creation, which now comes to an end. Soon the few animals and the angels will leave too. After fulfilling the prescription of the Jewish Law concerning first-born boys, Joseph and Mary will return to Nazareth. The brief account of an incident which happened when Jesus was twelve years old will alone be recorded, and then for more than twenty years there is silence.

The overture of Luke's Gospel comes to an end with no promise of immediate continuation. The symphony of God's peace on earth, struck up by the praise of the heavenly host and its echoes on earth, is not being played after all. The Jewish historian Josephus tells us about the horrors which happened immediately after Herod's death and how a militant Jewish movement began to fight against the occupying Roman army and the Jewish collaborators. This led to mass crucifixions of rebels. Most ancient Greek and Roman historians report nothing about what happened in Bethlehem. If they mention Jesus at all it is to record in passing that he was executed like many other Jewish rebels at that time.

What the historians do report at great length, however, is how the emperor Augustus extended the Roman peace as a true father of the nation and saviour of the world. In Antioch a coin was struck which showed on one side the god of heaven bringing victory and on the other the victorious Augustus with the inscription "worthy of honour", "son of God". After his death in A.D. 14 Caesar Augustus was indeed declared to be a divine being and was worshipped as such.

What did the young Jesus in Nazareth know of all those events on the scene of world history? How did he experience them? Nothing is known about all this. Later apocryphal childhood gospels tell fantastic and often cruel stories about Jesus as a wonder-working child and a small magician—all of them accounts of pious imagination.

When the canonical Gospels take up the story of Jesus again, no reference is made to the infancy narratives. Luke's Gospel could well have started in an earlier draft with the solemn beginning of chapter 3: "In the fifteenth year of the emperor Tiberius, when Pontius Pilate was governor of Judaea . . . the word of God came to John son of Zechariah in the wilderness" (Lk. 3:1–2). Caesar Tiberius inherited a position of power in imperial Rome. Compared to it the public ministry of Jesus started in a small, barely noticed way on the outskirts of the Roman empire. Tiberius had already retired to his villas of Capri, deeply depressed because of political intrigues, when, under that emperor's procurator in Palestine, Jesus finally received his crown and ascended his throne, but the crown was a crown of thorns and the throne that of the cross.

Should we then dismiss as a figment of pious imagination what Luke wrote in his first two chapters? Should we set aside what the angel of the Lord said, what the heavenly hosts sang and what a few pious Jews and nameless shepherds believed? There was one person who certainly did not do so: Mary. As one observes the facial expressions of the figures in Mlangeni's crib it becomes evident that she has imprinted in her heart and stamped on her memory all the things which had occurred and all that had been said and sung.

Mary: no other person except for her son Jesus has played a more central role in Christian piety and iconography than Mary. From the earliest times Christian believers wanted to know more about her than the New Testament accounts provided. Apocryphal writings from the 2nd century onwards try to fill this gap; they contain many details about her parents (identified as Joachim and Anna), her childhood and marriage.

The whole "Book of James", one of the earliest post-biblical infancy gospels, was written almost totally for the glorification of Mary. Like the Old Testament Hanna, Samuel's mother, so Anna, Joachim's wife, was without child and cried to the Lord. An angel appeared to her and said: "Anna, Anna, the Lord has heard your prayer. You shall conceive and bear, and your offspring shall be spoken of in the whole world." Immediately, Anna dedicated her future child to the Lord. When Mary "was six months old, her mother stood her on the ground to see if she could stand. And she walked (twice) seven steps and came back to her bosom. And she took her up, saying: 'As the Lord my God lives, you shall walk no more upon this ground until I take you into the temple of the Lord.' And she made a sanctuary of her bed-chamber, and did not permit anything common or unclean to pass through it."

Plate 19: *Christmas crib, sculptured by Alfred Mlangeni, South Africa. Contemporary.*

The "Book of James" then continues to tell stories about Mary's childhood. On her third birthday she was brought to the temple in a solemn procession and entrusted to the care of the priests. "And Mary was in the temple nurtured like a dove and received food from the hand of an angel." At twelve the priests betrothed her to the old widower Joseph whom a miraculous sign had designated as her husband. Later the lot fell to Mary to be the one to weave the part of "pure purple and scarlet" for the temple veil.

These stories and the legends that later developed around Mary have inspired many poets and painters during the Middle Ages. The ongoing theological reflection about the Theotokos (the one who gave birth to God) has influenced the prayer life of many Christians, especially among Eastern Orthodox and Roman Catholic believers. Such piety which centred on Mary also led to excesses. This in turn produced a strong Protestant reaction which tended to reject not only the post-biblical mariological affirmations but even the biblical testimony about Mary.

It is therefore important for all Christians of all confessions to listen together to what the evangelist Luke testifies about the mother of Jesus. When the angel of the Lord and the heavenly host had disappeared, and the shepherds took their leave, and things resumed their normal course, "Mary treasured all these things and pondered over them", "keeping them in her heart" (Lk. 2:19, 51).

With these verses Luke portrays Mary as the true disciple, anticipating the faithful church. She is in fact the only adult of the infancy narratives who continues to play a role in the two volumes of Luke's Gospel, both before and after the death and resurrection of Jesus.

Luke alone reports a revealing incident during Jesus' journey from Galilee to Jerusalem. While Jesus was teaching, suddenly a woman in the crowd called out: "Happy the womb that carried you and the breasts that suckled you!" Jesus does not deny the truth of this, but he points to a fuller truth: "Happy rather those who hear the Word of God and keep it" (Lk. 11:27f). The blessedness of Mary was her total readiness to hear and cherish God's Word. Thus she could make the link between Jesus'·childhood, his passion and resurrection and the life of the early Christians in Jerusalem. In this sense she prefigured the faithful church.

We do not know whether Mary was among the women "who had accompanied him from Galilee", were present at Jesus' crucifixion and burial, and later went to the empty tomb (Lk. 23:49, 55; 24:1). The evangelist John reports that the mother of Jesus stood under the cross (Jn 19:25ff), but Luke does not mention her by name in any of these texts. However, from the very beginning Mary was part of the gathering of disciples after Jesus' resurrection (Acts 1:14). Because she had not only memorized but deeply meditated in her heart on the things which had happened during the annunciation at Bethlehem and later in the temple of Jerusalem, she could understand something of what took place at Pentecost.

The verbs used by Luke for what Mary did ("to treasure up in the heart", "to ponder") recall the benediction in Psalm 1:

Happy are those whose delight is the Lord's Torah (that is his will, promise and guidance), those who meditate the Torah night and day (Ps. 1:1–2).

In the original Hebrew the verb usually translated by "to meditate" means literally "to murmur in a low voice". What has been memorized, internalized, pondered in the heart is again and again recalled and recited for oneself. This is exactly what Mary must have done, following an age-old Jewish custom.

Later the church fathers developed the notion and practice of the *ruminatio* on the basis of an allegorical interpretation of rumination among animals believed to be clean (Lev. 11:3; Deut. 14:6). Thus, with a sense of humour the Egyptian hermit St Anthony taught in the first half of the 4th century: "A camel needs only a little food; it keeps it within until it returns to the stable. It lets the food come up again and ruminates it until the food enters into the camel's bones and flesh. The horse, however, needs much food, it eats at all times and soon loses all it has eaten. So let us not be like a horse, continuously reciting the words of God without obeying any of them. Let us rather resemble the camel, reciting each word of God and retaining it within us until we have lived it."

St Anthony emphasized in this comparison the intimate relationship between the act of ruminating and the result of being penetrated by God's word to such an extent that it shapes our actions. Other authors describe the *ruminatio* more as a meditation which leads to new insights and continuous prayer. In his "Discipline for the Life of Ministers" Martin Luther gave the following advice (and since according to Luther all baptized Christians participate in the priesthood this advice is for all Christians): "In the evening, as you go to bed, by all means take a passage of holy scripture with you, know it by heart, and while you ruminate on it, you quietly fall asleep like a pure animal. This passage must not be too copious, but rather brief, yet well meditated and understood. And as you awake in the morning, you must find it back, like an inheritance from the past evening."

In the contemporary search for a sustaining spirituality, this ancient practice of the *ruminatio* needs to be rediscovered. Beset as we are by too many words and images, engaged in too many activities, impatient that there are too few immediate results, we must learn again to ruminate on God's word as Mary did. Writing about this way of meditation a sister of the Grandchamp community shows how memorization and the *ruminatio* are much more than a method. They call for an inner attitude leading to "a certain form of passivity which could well prove to be the highest form of human maturity". "Mary can help us to enter into this right attitude, to accept the state of a poor person who is fully open towards what is to come. What she receives into herself is not a new idea, an interesting discovery, but a life which will take form, which upsets her existence, a life which offers itself to her fragility."

Luke wrote the infancy narratives of Jesus not only so that we may read them. We must learn to keep and tell them, meditate upon them in our heart as Mary did. Then those stories will become part of our own life's story. And when we see Jesus not only in the manger, but also on the cross and as the risen Lord, we will understand how the overture and "symphony" of Luke's Gospel fit together. When we see the Spirit not only descending on the actors in the infancy narratives but also on people from many languages and cultures at Pentecost, we can ourselves become part of that history of salvation.

Matthew's teaching

1.

18. This is the story of the birth of the Messiah. Mary his mother was betrothed to Joseph; before their marriage she found that she was with child by

19. the Holy Spirit. Being a man of principle, and at the same time wanting to save her from exposure, Joseph desired to have the marriage contract set

20. aside quietly. He had resolved on this, when an angel of the Lord appeared to him in a dream. "Joseph son of David," said the angel, "do not be afraid to take Mary home with you as your wife. It is by the Holy Spirit that she has conceived this

21. child. She will bear a son; and you shall give him the name Jesus (Saviour), for he will save his people

22. from their sins." All this happened in order to fulfill what the Lord declared through the prophet: "The

23. virgin will conceive and bear a son, and he shall be called Emmanuel", a name which means "God is

24. with us". Rising from sleep Joseph did as the angel had directed him; he took Mary home to be his

25. wife, but had no intercourse with her until her son was born. And he named the child Jesus.

2.

1. Jesus was born at Bethlehem in Judaea during the reign of Herod. After his birth astrologers from the

2. east arrived in Jerusalem, asking, "Where is the child who is born to be king of the Jews? We observed the rising of his star, and we have come to

3. pay him homage." King Herod was greatly perturbed when he heard this; and so was the whole of

4. Jerusalem. He called a meeting of the chief priests and lawyers of the Jewish people, and put before them the question: "Where is it that the Messiah is

5. to be born?" "At Bethlehem in Judaea," they replied; and they referred him to the prophecy

6. which reads: "Bethlehem in the land of Judah, you are far from least in the eyes of the rulers of Judah; for out of you shall come a leader to be the shepherd of my people Israel."

7. Herod next called the astrologers to meet him in private, and ascertained from them the time when

8. the star had appeared. He then sent them on to Bethlehem, and said, "Go and make a careful inquiry for the child. When you have found him, report to me, so that I may go myself and pay him homage."

9. They set out at the king's bidding; and the star which they had seen at its rising went ahead of them until it stopped above the place where the child lay.

10. At the sight of the star they were overjoyed.

11. Entering the house, they saw the child with Mary his mother, and bowed to the ground in homage to him; then they opened their treasures and offered

12. him gifts: gold, frankincense, and myrrh. And being warned in a dream not to go back to Herod, they returned home another way.

13. After they had gone, an angel of the Lord appeared to Joseph in a dream, and said to him, "Rise up, take the child and his mother and escape with them to Egypt, and stay there until I tell you; for Herod is going to search for the child to do away with

14. him." So Joseph rose from sleep, and taking mother and child by night he went away with them to

15. Egypt, and there he stayed till Herod's death. This was to fulfill what the Lord had declared through the prophet: "I called my son out of Egypt."

Matthew 1:18–2:15

Matthew begins his Gospel in a strange way: "A table of descent of Jesus Christ, son of David, son of Abraham." And then comes that long list starting with "Abraham was the father of Isaac, Isaac of Jacob", etc. with the verb "begetting" appearing no fewer than forty times. It ends with: "Jacob was the father of Joseph, the husband of Mary, who gave birth to (or of whom was begotten) Jesus called Messiah" (Mt. 1:1–16). No wonder that with all these human begettings Matthew was assigned as evangelist's symbol the living creature "with a human face".

In the above graphic the symbolic companion of Matthew indicates to us by a gesture of the hand to pay attention. With this strange way of beginning a Gospel, with a theologically constructed genealogy, Matthew reveals to us at the very outset *who* Jesus is: he is the son of David, thus deeply rooted in the history of the people of Israel and bringing this history to its fulfilment as the expected messianic king of the house of David. He is also the son of Abraham, taking up and fulfilling the great promise that in the seed of Abraham all nations of the earth shall be blessed.

Having emphasized this significant human descent within the history of salvation, Matthew immediately goes on to stress the equally important divine descent of the Messiah. Indeed, *how* does Jesus enter human history? Not through the fatherhood of Joseph. An angel of the Lord appears to Joseph in a dream and reveals to him that the child to be born is conceived through the Holy Spirit by the virgin Mary (Mt. 1:18–25; see above pp. 32ff). It is in this connection that Matthew quotes the famous prophecy in Isaiah 7:14 and teaches us that Jesus received the title Immanuel which means "God with us".

The next part of Matthew's introductory chapters starts with the question of the Magi: "*Where* is the child who is born to be the king of the Jews?" They receive an amazing answer: not in Jerusalem, but in the village of Bethlehem! And an even more amazing thing happens: while the chief priests and learned scribes of the Jewish people do not go to worship the messianic king, these alien visitors immediately go to Bethlehem and prostrate themselves before the child—gentile astrologers, abhorrent sorcerers in the eyes of the Jews but sages in their own countries (Mt. 2:1–12).

A fourth question is asked: *Whence* does the Messiah come? One would expect the answer: "from Bethlehem". Jesus was not only born there, but according to Matthew's testimony Joseph has his home in that Judaean village. Yet Matthew lets God himself answer the question about the whence by once more quoting an Old Testament prophecy:

"Out of Egypt have I called my son!" Indeed, due to Herod's raving Jesus became a political refugee in Egypt. Even after Herod's death Joseph, Mary and the boy Jesus could not return to Judaea. They had to withdraw to the Galilee of the Gentiles, living as displaced persons in Nazareth, a village never mentioned in the Old Testament (Mt. 2:13–23).

Matthew's overture to the "symphony" of his gospel answers four basic questions about Jesus:
Who? —Son of David and Abraham, Son of God.
How? —By Joseph and the Holy Spirit.
Where? —In Bethlehem, city of the shepherd David.
Whence?—Out of Egypt, recalling the Exodus.

But who is this evangelist? And how do his infancy narratives anticipate the main themes of his gospel teaching?

A beautifully preserved stained glass window from the 13th century gives us part of the answer to these questions about Matthew and his good news. It forms part of the high and narrow windows above the south portal of the Cathedral at Chartres. The central window with Mary and the child is flanked on each side with windows portraying the four great prophets, each carrying on their shoulders one of the four evangelists. This manner of showing the intimate progression from the Old to the New Testament is rather exceptional in Christian iconography. It fits particularly well the evangelist Matthew who sits on the shoulders of Isaiah (Plate 20). More than any other evangelist Matthew constantly makes links with the Old Testament, quoting from or alluding to the Book of Isaiah alone over eighty times.

We do not know who this evangelist was. Nothing in his Gospel itself supports the ancient assumption that he was the tax-collector Matthew/Levi who became one of the twelve disciples. Had he been an eye-witness he would not need to be so heavily dependent on Mark who certainly was not an eye-witness. One might consider Matthew's Gospel as a second enlarged edition of the Gospel of Mark. Yet this does not do justice to the originality of Matthew. He also had access to the same oral or written source of the sayings of Jesus which Luke knew, and he too had gathered Jesus-traditions of his own. What characterizes Matthew most, however, is his reasoning from Scripture, a certain rabbinic flavour in his teaching.

Perhaps we get a glimpse of the author at the end of the kingdom parables. In a final comparison Jesus there tells his disciples about "a teacher of the law who has become a learner in the kingdom of heaven". He compares him with "a householder who can produce from his treasure both the new and old" (Mt. 13:52). Whether this is a discreet self-portrait of the evangelist or not, it is certainly an apt description of what he does with his gospel teaching. Many scholars indeed believe that Matthew was a converted Jewish rabbi, and that around A.D. 80 he taught somewhere in Syria. The church for which he wrote consisted probably of both Jewish and gentile Christians, still involved in a polemical debate about the Messiah with members of the Jewish synagogue across the street.

Again and again Matthew demonstrates that the Scriptures have been fulfilled in the words and acts, in the suffering and the final vindication through the resurrection of Christ, the Immanuel. This is not simply some new teaching added to the old one. Matthew does not stand beside the prophet Isaiah; he is carried by the latter on his shoulders. The evangelist has thus a wider horizon, he can see further and perceive new events which change the whole perspective. In fact, the householder of Jesus' parable does not take out of his treasure the old and the new, as Matthew is often misquoted. The new precedes the old. An all-decisive new event has happened which alters the old perception: the Messiah has come, and he came in a totally unexpected way as the suffering Messiah! In the light of this new event Matthew rereads and reinterprets the Law and the prophets.

Jesus says in the Sermon on the Mount: "You have learned that our forefathers were told . . . But what I tell you is this . . ." Only Moses could speak with such an authority, and Matthew presents Jesus indeed as a new Moses. Already in his introductory chapters Matthew develops a striking parallelism between the infancy narratives of Moses and of Jesus (compare below pp. 85ff).

The portrayal of Jesus as a new Moses has perhaps affected the whole structure of Matthew's Gospel. After the genealogy the infancy narratives consist of five scenes, each built around an Old Testament quotation.

They are artfully put together so as to mirror one another. The second and fourth scene show how Herod reacts to the birth of Jesus in Bethlehem, while the remaining three scenes deal with divine commands which Joseph receives in a dream:

Mt. 1:18–25	Isa. 7:14	Joseph's dream: accept Mary!
Mt. 2: 1–12	Micah 5:2	Herod, Magi, Bethlehem.
Mt. 2:13–15	Hos. 11:1	Joseph's dream: to Egypt!
Mt. 2:16–18	Jer. 31:15	Herod, children, Bethlehem.
Mt. 2:19–23	(uncertain)	Joseph's dream: to Nazareth!

Many scholars see before the concluding passion and resurrection accounts a similar five-fold pattern in the main body of Matthew's Gospel. Each section starts with a miscellaneous group of sayings and episodes, leads up to a major teaching by Jesus and concludes with a typical sentence ("when Jesus had finished this discourse, he left . . .").

Mt. 3:1–7:29	with the Sermon on the Mount.
Mt. 8:1–11:1	with the instructions for the mission to Jews.
Mt. 11:2–13:53	with the teaching by parables of the kingdom.
Mt. 13:54–19:1	with the instructions about church life.
Mt. 19:2–26:1	with the warnings about the final judgment.

This reconstruction of Matthew's teachings may be artificial. If, however, the evangelist consciously created this structure he thereby showed that with the Messiah Jesus a new Pentateuch, a new five books of Moses concerning God's promises and instructions, was established.

The coming of the Magi in the infancy narratives forms another anticipation of a major emphasis in Matthew's teaching. Before his resurrection Jesus limits his mission strictly to the Jewish people. Yet the first who come to pay homage to him are the gentile Magi. Later other Gentiles come to implore Jesus' help, a Canaanite woman and even the Roman military commander of Capernaum (Mt. 15:21ff; 8:5ff). As will be shown later (compare p. 76) this leads to a fundamental change in God's mission policy. For there is this great paradox to which Matthew points in his Gospel, already in the story of the Magi: the one who came to be the Messiah and Immanuel for his own people was rejected by the leaders of the Jews, while total outsiders were coming to worship him. Therefore, after the vindication of resurrection, Jesus' Jewish-Christian followers are sent out to the nations (Mt. 28:16–20).

Just as Jesus had preceded his disciples in his ministry to the Jewish people, so he precedes them now in the world-wide mission to the Gentiles. No ascension story

Plate 20: *Prophet/evangelist window (Isaiah with Matthew), Cathedral in Chartres, France. 13th century.*

concludes Matthew's Gospel. Jesus remains with us: "Be assured, I am with you always, to the end of time!" With this last sentence of the Gospel, the title Immanuel, given to Jesus at the beginning of Matthew's teaching, is taken up again and revealed in its universal significance: Jesus is "God with us" not only for the Jewish people and Palestine, but he becomes the Immanuel for all nations in the whole universe.

The astrologers

For people in the ancient world it was not strange that a star should herald the birth of a king. Jewish, Greek and Latin sources of the time of Matthew often reported such extraordinary phenomena. Yet, despite detailed astronomical studies concerning exceptional celestial phenomena around the time of the birth of Jesus, conducted since Johannes Kepler in the 17th century, no one has so far discovered anything that quite fits the "star of Bethlehem". It is true that in 7 or 6 B.C. three planets could be observed in a constellation unusually close to one another (Mars, Jupiter and Saturn). This might well have puzzled astrologers in Persia or Babylon.

Nor was it strange to the first readers of Matthew's Gospel that astrologers from the East would actually come to search for the king announced by such a constellation of stars. Roman historians report how in A.D. 66 the king of Armenia, Tiridates, created quite a stir when he came to Rome to pay homage to the emperor Nero: "I have come to you, my god, to pay homage, as I do to Mithras" (Mithras is a Persian divinity). Tiridates and his companions were actually called Magi, and the historians add that "the king did not return by the route he had followed in coming".

Such reports do not prove the historicity of Matthew's story. They show, however, that on the basis of observed natural phenomena and recorded historical events, stories like this could easily develop in the church's oral tradition about Jesus, even more so if such stories confirmed beliefs and prophecies of the Old Testament. No doubt Matthew believed that what he wrote had actually happened, and no scholar can scientifically prove that the main features of the story of the Magi could not have taken place. It was not however the historicity of such events, but their theological significance which excited the churches' curiosity and which led to the inclusion of this particular story in Matthew's infancy narratives.

What then is its theological significance? Much depends on one's approach to the Magi. There is a biblical, Jewish and early Christian tradition which sees in the Magi abhorrent charlatans and sorcerers. Simon, a Jewish magus, is portrayed as one who wants to buy the power of God's Spirit and must repent of his wickedness (Acts 8:18ff). This was how the apostle Paul confronted the magus Elymas in Cyprus: "You swindler, you rascal, son of the devil and enemy of all goodness, will you never stop falsifying the straight ways of the Lord?" (Acts 13:10). Seen in this light, the Magi are in Jewish and Christian eyes prototypes of non-believers, the most unlikely persons to become true worshippers of God. And yet—according to Matthew's testimony—*they* were the first who came to worship Christ.

If the Magi are understood as such prototypes of unbelievers, Matthew's account of their coming to the child born to be king becomes a conversion story. In Jesus' presence all magic powers are overthrown. This scene recalls then the Egyptian magicians who were defeated by the superior miraculous power which worked through Aaron and Moses (Ex. 7:8–13). Yet in the exodus story Pharaoh, and presumably his magicians as well, remained obstinate, while in Matthew's account the Magi fell prostrate before Jesus.

It has even been suggested that the "presents" of gold, frankincense and myrrh were not gifts at all, but tools for sorcery which the Magi deposited at the feet of Jesus as a sign of submission. This is the interpretation given in Ian M. Fraser's poem about the Magi:

Magi versed in secret lore,
note strange portents in the sky.
The Fiend to appease?
Evil transcendent?
—the omen sublime
a Child Ascendent!
   Camels saddled, tools of trade
   packed, they trace a path star-made,
   eyes fixed high, discarding their charts.

Questions shake Jerusalem
(voiceless myrrh, frankincense, gold)
"Where's the Great Lord
whose heralded birth
displaces the stars
unhinges the earth?"
   Priests and scribes consult, agree:
   Herod says "I'll bend the knee—
   southward hold, to Bethlehem."

Rapt, they face the world's one Light.
Changed, they cast before the Son,
gold, the seducer,
death-witching myrrh,
priestly mystique limned
in smoke from the fir
   broken is the Devil's sway:
   warned, they choose a different way.
   Life is begun, the blind have sight!

The interpretation of the story of the Magi as symbolizing the overthrow of all magic appears very early in church history. Ignatius, the bishop of Antioch, wrote around A.D. 110 in his letter to the Ephesians: "A star, brighter than all other stars, shone in the sky . . .

Thereupon all magic was dissolved, every bond of malice disappeared, ignorance was destroyed, the ancient kingdom was ruined, when God appeared in the form of man to give us newness of life."

The Magi as astrologers or priests who come to submit themselves to Jesus is a favourite theme in early Christian art. Long before the shepherds appeared on the Christmas scenes, even before the earliest portrayals of the nativity with Jesus in the crib with the ox and the donkey behind him were sculptured or painted, the coming of the Magi was portrayed, from as early as the 3rd century onwards. Some ten times they appear in the catacombs and as often on early Christian sarcophagi, dressed with Persian or Parthian belted tunics and with Phrygian caps.

The models for such portrayals were the artistic representations of Graeco-Roman antiquity which show a delegation of defeated barbarians coming to the victorious general or emperor, bringing a golden wreath as a sign of submission. Mary, sitting in a stately chair and holding the boy Jesus on her knees, replaced the general or emperor. The defeated barbarians have now become the Magi on their way to Jesus. Or they are presented as already arrived before Mary and the infant-king.

Often other biblical episodes are combined with the coming of the Magi, like the Old Testament story of the three Jewish young men Shadrach, Meshach and Abednego who refused to worship the image of king Nebuchadnezzar in Babylon (Dan. 3). The point of Matthew's story is thus enhanced by Daniel's story: no earthly ruler is to be worshipped, be it Nebuchadnezzar, Herod or the Roman emperor. Only to God and the Immanuel is worship due.

An early Christian sarcophagus shows on its left side another significant juxtaposition (Plate 21). As in the above quotation from Ignatius, the universal significance of Matthew's teaching about the Magi is emphasized. On the lower level the Magi arrive before Mary and her son. Jesus takes hold of the golden wreath. Behind Mary stands the prophet Balaam who had spoken of the rising star. The first Magus points to the three stars above Jesus and Mary while the other two fix their eyes on the stars. On the upper level the creation of Adam and Eve is portrayed, and the two receive symbols of their work: Adam sheafs of corn for work in the field and Eve a lamb for weaving wool. Yet this image of paradise is poisoned by the snake and the human revolt against God. What went wrong in creation will now be set right by the Immanuel. Jesus is thus seen here as the new Adam and the son of Abraham, through whom blessing comes to all the nations. A sign of this blessing is portrayed in the healing of the blind child on the right side of the Magi.

With the coming of the Immanuel a new era has begun. This is proclaimed during the Christmas vespers in the Orthodox Church in the following prayer:

Your nativity, O Christ our God,
has shone upon the world with the light of knowledge:
for thereby they who adored the stars
through a star were taught to worship You,
the Sun of Righteousness, and to know You,
the Dayspring from on high. O Lord, glory to You!

Plate 21: *Clipeus sarcophagus (detail). Rome. Ca. 315.*

The kings

The story of the Magi is often told and portrayed as the story of the three kings. There appear indeed kings in this narrative, but only two and not three. And the persons designated by the Greek title *basileus*, king, are not the Magi, but Herod and Jesus. Already in the ancient church, however, the Magi were sometimes identified as kings, though only from the 10th century onwards do they appear as such in Christian iconography. Two such Magi/kings are reproduced in Plate 22 which is one of the 153 painted panels on the ceiling of the small St Martin's church in Zillis.

The dramatic confrontation between the mighty king Herod and the vulnerable infant-king Jesus received little attention in the church's meditation on this passage. Almost immediately the interest centred on the intriguing personalities of the Magi. In the biblical text itself nothing is said about their number. Both in early Christian writing and iconography one finds different numbers: two visitors from the East appear in the catacombs of St Peter and St Marcellus, three in the Priscilla catacombs and four in the catacomb of St Domitilla. A Syrian tradition even speaks about twelve Magi. However, on the basis of the three gifts (Mt. 2:11) three soon became the accepted number. The Romanesque panels of Zillis show in fact three Magi-kings, the two reproduced in Plate 22 and the third already before Mary and the boy Jesus on an adjacent panel.

As early as the end of the 2nd century the Latin church father Tertullian reported that "the East considers Magi almost as kings". From where did they get this royal status? As was often the case, and is in fact quite in keeping with Matthew's teaching, the story of the Magi was seen as the fulfilment of several Old Testament prophecies. Matthew does not actually quote these texts, but they may well have been in his mind. To Jerusalem it is promised:

*The riches of the sea shall be lavished upon you
and you shall possess the wealth of nations.
Camels in droves shall cover the land,
dromedaries of Midian and Ephah,
all coming from Sheba
laden with golden spice and frankincense,
heralds of the Lord's praise* (Isa. 60:5f).

To the Davidic king the promise is made:

*The kings of Tarshish and the islands shall bring gifts,
the kings of Sheba and Seba shall present their tribute,
and all kings shall pay him homage,
all nations shall serve him* (Ps. 72:10f).

What had been announced in these and other texts about Jerusalem and the Davidic king was seen as fulfilled by the coming of the Magi with their gifts.

Once the Magi were identified as kings, Christian imagination worked overtime. Many varying legends about the names and origins, the destinies and deaths of these Magi/kings began to circulate. In the West the following description had great influence on later Christian art. It is probably wrongly assigned to the Anglo-Saxon historian Bede (Beda Venerabilis, ca. 700): "The Magi were the ones who gave gifts to the Lord. The first is said to have been Melchior, an old man with white hair and a long beard . . . who offered gold to the Lord as to a king. The second, Gaspar by name, young and beardless and ruddy complexioned . . . honoured him as God by his gift of incense, an oblation worthy of divinity. The third, black-skinned and heavily bearded, named Balthasar . . . by his gift of myrrh testified to the Son of Man who was to die."

Whether Matthew thought of the Magi also as kings or not, this clearly was not the main emphasis of his teaching. He did not quote the passages from Isaiah 60 and Psalm 72, but in the story of the Magi he referred to prophecies in Micah and 2 Samuel. The kings for him were in the first place the mighty king Herod and, confronting him, the infant-king Jesus.

King Herod was a fascinating personality. Son of the adventurer Antipas, a descendant from the Edomites, young Herod began his career as a successful military commander against rebels in Galilee. A contemporary of Matthew, the Jewish historian Josephus, reports that "in all Syrian villages and towns Herod's praises were sung, because he had won back for them their peace and property". A shrewd politician, Herod gained the friendship of the Roman general Mark Antony, and later became a protégé of the great emperor Augustus. From 37–4 B.C. he ruled under the Romans as king of the Jews and extended his domain till it was almost the size of the kingdom of David and Solomon.

While defending the Jews and their religion, Herod also introduced Greek and Roman styles of life to Palestine. He was a great builder. The temple in Jerusalem was rebuilt from 20 or 19 B.C. onwards. Many fortresses were erected, and even whole cities with palaces and sports arenas. This brought peace to Palestine

Plate 22: *Two Magi/kings, painted panel on ceiling of St Martin's church, Zillis, Switzerland. First half of 12th century.*

and employment opportunities, but it also led to heavy taxation and a harsh rule with secret police and arbitrary executions.

Not being a Jew Herod could not claim to be the rightful successor of David or the expected messianic king. He therefore became deeply suspicious of any Jews who might revolt against him. Towards the end of his life he suffered from a persecution mania, and the intrigues surrounding his succession led to an explosive situation.

No wonder that Herod was "greatly perturbed", and with him the whole of Jerusalem, when the visitors from the East enquired about the "child born to be king of the Jews". Of course Herod had all the military power. But the infant-king Jesus represented an authority which no sword could fight.

Probably the evangelist had come across the story of the Magi in the oral tradition of the church. He added to it, however, references to the Old Testament (Mt. 2:6), thereby helping discerning readers to see the theological significance of the story. The first part of the quotation is taken from Micah 5:2, the prophecy about Bethlehem and its significance in Jewish messianic expectations (compare above pp. 50ff). Linked with this is a quotation from 2 Samuel 5:2, dealing with the anointing of David, ruler of Judah in Hebron, as king over the whole people of Israel, by the elders of the tribes of Israel.

Matthew suggests that the Jewish scribes unconsciously "confess" Jesus as the expected Messiah through referring to these Old Testament passages. The genealogy stating that Jesus is "son of Abraham" has been confirmed by the coming of the gentile astrologers (compare above pp. 67ff). Now the Old Testament quotation establishes the other important aspect of the heritage of Jesus: he is "son of David". Herod can destroy the children in Bethlehem whom later the church will recognize as the first Christian martyrs. But just as the boy Moses was rescued from the slaughter of Hebrew boys by the Egyptian Pharaoh, so the boy Jesus is rescued from king Herod's wrath—and paradoxically he finds refuge in Egypt!

The sages

Are the Magi in Matthew's Gospel astrologers, and therefore in the eyes of early Christians abhorrent sorcerers—in which case they are the most unlikely group of Gentiles to come and worship the Immanuel? Or do they represent the kings of the nations who, according to Old Testament promises, come to pay homage and bring gifts to the King of kings? Both interpretations are possible (compare above pp. 67ff and 70). But a third interpretation is even closer to the original narrative.

Though not explicitly quoted, the strange visions and prophecies of Balaam must have been in the minds of those who first told the story of the Magi, probably also in the mind of Matthew when he included this narrative in his Gospel. Balak, the ruler of the Moabites, did not want to let the Israelites pass through his country on their way to Canaan. He therefore called on the famous seer Balaam "from the East" to put a curse on the Israelites. Instead of cursing, Balaam pronounced blessings. He even made the following prophecy:

I see him, but not now:
I behold him, but not near:
a star shall come forth out of Jacob,
a comet arise from Israel.
He shall smite the squadrons of Moab
and beat down all the sons of strife.
Edom shall be his by conquest (Num. 24:17f).

In the time of Jesus, Balaam was considered by some to have been a Magus, and the prophecy about the star was understood as a pointer to the coming messianic King. The story about the Magi thus recalled in many ways the figure of Balaam. Like the Magi he came from the East. He saw from afar the messianic King whom the Magi now worshipped. A bright star is central in both stories. Balaam acted against the evil plans of the Moabite king Balak who parallels the "Edomite" king Herod.

In the Book of Numbers Balaam is described as a good Gentile and an instrument of God who prophesied well for the Israelites. After his mission was accomplished he did not become an Israelite, but—like the Magi—he "returned home". The Magi can thus be seen as true sages from among the Gentiles. With their own wisdom, in this case their astrological knowledge, they found the way towards the Immanuel, though at the last stop-over of their journey they had to be helped by pointers from the revelation in the Hebrew scriptures. Again the biblical text does not indicate that the Magi became Christians. Having prostrated themselves before the king Jesus "they returned home another way".

The Old Testament is usually summed up as "the law and the prophets", yet it contains a third very important strand, the Wisdom tradition. It appears most clearly in the Proverbs, the Ecclesiastes and many Psalms, but it had also a strong influence on the writing of history among the Israelites, starting under king Solomon. Typical for this Wisdom tradition is its openness to the wisdom of other cultures which it often borrowed from or adapted. Egyptian and Babylonian proverbs are thus freely quoted and incorporated into the wisdom which Israelites gained as they walked according to God's command and promise. A stylistic device in Wisdom teaching is to state alternative ways of life, showing their consequences, at the same time letting people free to make their own responsible choices.

Matthew has been strongly influenced by this Wisdom tradition. According to his testimony Jesus taught like a Wisdom teacher, placing before us a whole series of alternatives: Are we going through the large or the narrow door? Do we build on sand or on stone? Shall we belong to the foolish or wise girls, to the sheep or the goats? (Mt. 7:13ff, 24ff; 25:1ff, 31ff). Right at the beginning and at the end of his Gospel, Matthew faces us with the most decisive choices: Are we to choose the mighty king Herod or the vulnerable infant-king Jesus? Will we join the mission with a lie, propagated by the chief priests, or the mission of the good news, following the risen Lord who precedes us (Mt. 2:1–12; 28:11–20)? The Queen of the South was the wise one: "She came from the ends of the earth to hear the wisdom of Solomon; and what is here (the Messiah) is greater than Solomon!" (Mt. 12:42, compare 11:19 where Jesus intimates that through his work God's wisdom is vindicated, that in him this wisdom becomes incarnate.)

We can thus well imagine that Matthew would be very sensitive to the story which tells about sages. Like his master he was himself a good Wisdom teacher. He must have found great delight in including the narrative of the Magi in his Gospel, showing how gentile sages found their way to the Immanuel, in whom God's wisdom appeared.

For thousands of years wisdom has been learned and taught in China. Many a Chinese print shows a sage sitting under a tree near a brook, looking at the mountain ranges beyond while meditating on the old wisdom sayings which he has drawn with calligraphy on a scroll. No wonder that in the Chinese Christian art of the first half of this century the coming of the sages to Jesus and Jesus as a Wisdom teacher are favourite subjects.

From its very beginning in A.D. 635, when the Nestorian missionary A-lo-pen came to China, Chinese

Christianity had sought to relate the old Chinese wisdom to the new Christian faith. "A virgin bore a Sage" is the oldest summary of the Christmas story as it was told in China. It appears on the famous Nestorian tablet which was erected in A.D. 781. The top part of this tablet is reproduced on Plate 23. The inscription reads: "The Tablet of the spread of the Ta Ch'in (Syrian) illustrious Religion in China". Beneath this title (and not reproduced on Plate 23) is engraved in beautiful small calligraphy a summary of the faith and a history of this first church in China. It is a strange blend of Syrian Christian and old Chinese wisdom. This has been visually portrayed in the adorned cross, which stands on a lotus flower. It is surrounded by clouds issuing from the base of the cross. As lord Buddha sits on the lotus, and as in China the wisdom of sages is often symbolized by clouds, Jesus has here been portrayed on the throne of the lotus and surrounded by wisdom.

The Nestorian tablet confesses the Immanuel in these words:

Some point to the creature,
to trust in it as the ultimate.
Some take things and nothingness,
and destroy the two.
Some pray and sacrifice to induce blessings.
Some set forth their own merit to deceive others.
Wise counsels were a-buzz.

Thoughts and feelings were a-toil.
Far and wide (they went) without achievement.
The dry hastened to turn to burning.
As darkness gathered they lost their way,
until confusion was beyond return.
Whereupon our Trinity became incarnate:
The Illustrious Honoured-One, Messiah,
hid away his true majesty,
and came into the world as a man.
An angel proclaimed the joy.
A virgin bore a Sage in Syria.
A bright star was the propitious portent.
Persians saw its glory and came to offer gifts.
He fulfilled the Old Law
of the Twenty-Four Sages' discourses,[1]
governing tribes and nation . . .
He determined the salvation of the Eight Stages,[2]
refining the earthly and perfecting the heavenly.
He revealed the gate of the Three Constants,[3]
unfolding life and destroying death.
He hung a brilliant sun
which scattered the regions of darkness.
The Devil's guile, lo, he has utterly cut off.

[1] The Old Testament.
[2] The Beatitudes.
[3] Probably the three commandments of Mt. 22:37ff and Mt. 7:12, as quoted in Didache 1:2 (an early Christian church order).

Plate 23: *Nestorian tablet of Hsi-An (detail), with oldest Chinese Christian cross and summary of history and faith of First Chinese Church. Erected in A.D. 781.*

大秦景教流行中國碑

The coming of the Gentiles

Haitian art was virtually unknown until the 1940s. Then suddenly there was an outburst of creativity, mainly by Haitians who had never followed any formal training. Today their work is acknowledged as the most amazing "art naïf" of our time.

Religious subjects and visions predominate. The mixture of mainly Roman Catholic popular piety and African religious heritage is often intriguing. Many of these works of art are clearly syncretistic; they mix Christian faith with Afro-American cults like that of the voodoo. But perhaps this expresses the mixed faith of the Magi, and of many Christians in all continents today though they usually are not aware of it. Therefore the church needs in our time the gospel teaching of the evangelist Matthew as much as it did in the 1st century.

Haitian art became known mainly for its brightly coloured paintings, but there are also remarkable sculptures like the one by Nacius Joseph (Plate 24) which shows the coming of animals and of gentile sages/kings to the infant Immanuel.

Matthew's Gospel forms the link between the Old and the New Testament (compare above pp. 63ff). This becomes apparent also in what the evangelist teaches about Christ and the nations. According to the Old Testament, the Israelites were not chosen for a mission of proclaiming a message to the Gentiles and for bringing them into their own community. God rather elected his people for a presence among the nations. This presence receives its special quality by three callings. First, God's people must worship the Lord who had entered into an intimate covenant relationship with them. Second, God's people must obey the will of this Lord and walk according to Torah, the commandments and promises. Third, God's people must live by hope. This hope includes the expectation that in the messianic age the Gentiles will come to Zion, as the prophet Isaiah had announced:

All the nations shall come streaming to it,
and many peoples shall come and say,
"Come, let us climb up on to the mountain of the Lord,
to the house of the God of Jacob,
that he may teach us his ways
and we may walk in his paths."
For instruction issues from Zion,
and out of Jerusalem comes the word of the Lord (Isa. 2:2–3).

Matthew maintains this Old Testament expectation. He affirms in his Gospel that in Jesus of Nazareth the Messiah has come and, therefore, the pilgrimage of the nations to Zion now begins. Yet the goal of the journey is no more a mountain or a city. God's path leads to a person: to Jesus. His name reveals that he is the one "who will save his people from their sins" (Mt. 1:21); He is "called Immanuel, a name which means 'God with us'" (Mt. 1:23). Therefore it was a mistake when the Magi went to mount Zion, to Jerusalem. The Messiah had been born not in Herod's palace, but in a house at Bethlehem. The one who can teach God's way, who communicates God's word by his whole life and death, is the child in the crib. In Nacius Joseph's sculpture, all the eyes, of Joseph and Mary and of the Magi and the animals, are therefore fixed on him.

The story of the Magi shows that the coming of the Gentiles begins with the birth of the Messiah. This theme of Matthew's overture reappears throughout the "symphony" of his Gospel. A Roman army officer comes to Jesus; his faith is so profound that Jesus exclaims: "I tell you this: nowhere, even in Israel, have I found such faith! Many, I tell you, will come from east and west to feast with Abraham, Isaac, and Jacob in the kingdom of Heaven" (Mt. 8:10f). There are other instances of this coming of the Gentiles: the Queen of the South who, long before Jesus' times, came to seek wisdom from the Davidic king Solomon; the Canaanite woman who forces her way into the presence of Jesus and literally throws herself at his feet (Mt. 12:42; 15:21–28). The climax comes at the moment of Jesus' death on the cross. Once again a Roman army officer *and* the Roman legionaries (only Matthew adds to the centurion: "and his men who were keeping watch") acknowledge the crucified rabbi as "God's son" (Mt. 27:54).

However, this movement of the Gentiles towards Jesus during his life-time was only an anticipation of the expected streaming of all the nations to the Messiah. Taking up the language of Jesus' parable about the wedding of the king's son, which Matthew interprets as the great messianic feast (Mt. 22:1–10), one might say that all guests, both Jewish and gentile, have been slow in coming.

The story of the wedding feast points to the change in God's mission policy. While in Luke's Gospel it is a straightforward parable (Lk. 14:16–24), in Matthew's version it becomes an allegorical summary of the history of salvation: twice the king sends out servants to call those who had been invited to the marriage feast (probably an allusion to the commissioning of the Old Testament prophets and of Jesus' disciples to the Jewish people). Yet those invited do not respond. They even

Plate 24: "Adoration", wood-sculpture by Nacius Joseph, Haiti. Contemporary.

ill-treat the royal servants. The king therefore sent troops and "set their town on fire" (almost certainly an allusion to the destruction of Jerusalem in A.D. 70). "Then he said to his servants: The wedding-feast is ready; but the guests I invited did not deserve the honour. Go out (the same verb as the one used in Mt. 28:19) to the main thoroughfares, and invite everyone you can find to the wedding."

This refers to the world-wide mission. According to Matthew's teaching the risen Lord had preceded his disciples to Galilee, and there, from a mountain, he sends them out to prepare and invite the nations for the messianic feast: "Full authority in heaven and on earth has been committed to me. Go forth therefore and make all nations my disciples; baptize people everywhere in the name of the Father and the Son and the Holy Spirit, and teach them to observe all that I have commanded you" (Mt. 28:18ff).

No wonder that the ancient feast of Epiphany on the 6th of January does not relate the coming of the Magi primarily to the nativity of Jesus. It is celebrated as the manifestation, the *epiphaneia*, of Christ among the nations. Hence the collect for this day in the Roman mass:

On this day, Lord God,
by a guiding star you revealed your only-begotten Son
to all the peoples of the world.
Lead us from the faith by which we know you now
to the vision of your glory, face to face.
We make this prayer through our Lord.

Joseph's dream

*An angel of the Lord appeared
to Joseph in a dream.*

One might well ask: Which Joseph? Was it the ancient patriarch who not only dreamt dreams but knew how to interpret them? Or was it the husband of Mary who brought her and Jesus to Egypt where the patriarch had lived? In several scenes of Matthew's infancy narratives one can indeed detect an underlying parallelism between the Old Testament patriarch Joseph (compare Gen. 37; 40; 45f; Ex. 1) and the New Testament Joseph, the legal father of Jesus.

Both had much to do with dreams. Both came to Egypt because of an emergency, the first because he was sold by his brothers, the second because he and his family had to escape a massacre of children. Both found refuge in Egypt. When there was a severe famine in Canaan, the patriarch Joseph could not only sell Egyptian corn to his brothers; he could invite them and his old father Jacob, helping them to "go down to Egypt" to escape starvation. The second Joseph had to safeguard the boy Jesus from the evil ruler Herod, just as before him the descendants of the patriarch Joseph had to safeguard their own boys from the evil Pharaoh "who knew nothing about Joseph".

The husband of Mary had thus a destiny similar to that of his famous namesake and ancestor. This meant also that Jesus relived part of the Israelite history and found refuge in Egypt.

Contrary to Luke's infancy narratives, where Mary has the chief role, it is Joseph who receives divine revelations in Matthew's account. Through Joseph's genealogy Jesus is son of David and Abraham (Mt. 1:1ff). Presented as "a man of principles", literally an "upright" or "just" one (Mt. 1:19), Joseph plans to act in a delicate situation both according to the law and with mercy towards Mary.

Jewish marriage procedures at that time had two stages: there was a formal exchange of consent before witnesses which meant much more than simply an exchange of promise as in modern betrothals. This first step was legally binding, though the husband and wife did not yet live together. The second step, namely the taking of the bride into the husband's family home,

could take place years later. When, after the formal exchange of consent, it appeared that Mary was with child, following the requirements of law Joseph decided not to marry her, but without exposing her to public disgrace.

At that point an angel of the Lord intervened and in a dream announced to Joseph, not to Mary, the extra-ordinary conception of the child: "Joseph, son of David, do not be afraid to take Mary home with you as your wife. It is by the Holy Spirit that she has conceived this child" (Mt. 1:20). And Joseph does what he is asked to do.

In Matthew's account there are two other occasions when the same sequence of events occurs:

—A situation arises where a vital decision must be taken
—An angel of the Lord appears to Joseph in a dream
—Joseph receives through the angel a divine command, together with the reason for it
—Joseph unhesitatingly obeys, "getting up", "taking the child and his mother", and thus providing security (Mt. 2:13–14 and 2:19–21).

It is only in the narrative about the Magi and the related account of the murder of children in Bethlehem that Joseph does not appear. Otherwise he is constantly on the scene, making decisions and taking action.

After the Magi had gone home, "an angel of the Lord appeared to Joseph in a dream, and said to him, 'Rise up, take the child and his mother and escape with them to Egypt' . . . So Joseph rose from sleep, and taking mother and child by night he went away with them to Egypt" (Mt. 2:13f). As Joseph plays such an important role in Matthew's infancy narratives it is appropriate that he should carry the boy Jesus on his shoulders.

The portrayal of the flight to Egypt, as it appears on the illumination in an Ethiopian gospel book (Plate 25), is rare in Christian iconography. Yet the unknown artist of this painting must have well studied Matthew's teaching. Joseph here leads the way and carries the load.

The earliest visual interpretations of the flight to Egypt show, from the 6th century onwards, Mary riding side-saddle on a donkey. She holds the boy Jesus who sits enthroned on her knees, while Joseph usually guides the donkey. Soon additional figures appear. Sometimes a young man carries water-skins and wood or guides the donkey. This is either a servant or a son from the supposed first marriage of Joseph, as reported in apocryphal gospels. According to legends it was James, the brother of Jesus, who later played such an important role in the early church.

In other portrayals of the flight, like the one in Plate 25, a woman accompanies the holy family. Usually she is identified as Salome who, according to the apocryphal infancy Gospel of James (2nd century), was present at Jesus' birth. During the journeys of the holy family in Egypt a young girl is said to have accompanied them. This is what an Arabic infancy gospel, translated from a lost Syriac original of the 4th or 5th century, affirms: "The woman took sweet-smelling water to wash the Lord Jesus; when she had washed him, she kept that water . . . and poured some of it upon a girl who lived there and whose body was white with leprosy . . . Immediately the girl was cleansed of the leprosy. And the inhabitants of that town said: 'There is no doubt that Joseph and Mary and this child are gods, not men'. And when they prepared to depart from them, that girl who had suffered from leprosy came to them, and asked them to take her with them as a companion."

Such later legendary additions must not detract our attention from Matthew's sober account and his insistence on the very human Joseph.

The Roman Catholic Church celebrates the Saint Joseph feast on the 19th of March. In one of the prescribed readings for the celebration, taken from a sermon of St Bernadine of Siena (15th century), the significance of Joseph for the coming of the Immanuel is expressed in the following way:

A comparison can be made between Joseph and the whole church of Christ. Joseph was the specially chosen man through whom and under whom Christ entered the world fittingly and in an appropriate way. So, if the whole church is in the debt of the Virgin Mary, since, through her, it was able to receive the Christ, surely after her, it also owes to Joseph special thanks and veneration. For he it is who marks the closing of the Old Testament. In him the dignity of the prophets and patriarchs achieves its promised fulfilment.

Plate 25: *"Flight to Egypt", illumination from the Gospel book of King David (1508–1540), Ethiopia. Early 16th century.*

Egypt, the land of refuge

For many centuries the crucifixion was not portrayed in terms of suffering, but as Jesus' victory and enthronement. Similarly the early interpretations of Jesus' flight to Egypt present it not as an escape from a massacre, but as a triumphal imperial departure for conquest. Iconography was thus strongly influenced by the many legends which soon began to overgrow the few sentences in Matthew's story, some of them quite endearing, others more fantastic.

The Arabic infancy gospel, to which we have already referred, contains the famous story of the two robbers, the good Titus and the evil Dumachus, whom Jesus identified as the two robbers with whom he would be crucified. It also tells about the children who had been changed into goats and whom Jesus changed back into boys and girls so that he could play with them.

The Gospel of Pseudo-Matthew (with material from the 4th to the 8th centuries) includes the legend of the lions and leopards which worshipped Jesus, going before the holy family to guide them on the way. They "showed their servitude by wagging their tails and honoured him with great reverence". When Mary was hungry and thirsty, resting in the shadow of a tall palm tree, Jesus ordered the tree to bend down, so that the family could refresh themselves with its fruits and drink from the water which began miraculously to flow from under the tree. Upon Jesus' command the tree straightened itself, and an angel was ordered to transplant one of its branches in paradise. Jesus also shortened the way through the scorching desert, so that a thirty-day stretch could be done in a single day.

Such legends are often reported as fulfilments of Old Testament prophecies. The journey through the desert is related to earlier journeys of the Israelites, to the creation stories and the hope for cosmic peace. Jesus thus manifests himself as the Lord over all creation.

This triumphal view of the "flight" to Egypt appears most clearly in the many legends about the arrival of the holy family in Egypt, often portrayed in medieval Christian art. The following episode from Pseudo-Matthew was so popular that it became one of the few non-biblical stories about Jesus to be included in the *Biblia pauperum* (cf. above p. 29):

Happy and rejoicing they came to the region of Hermopolis, and entered an Egyptian city called Sotinen. And since there was in it no one they knew whom they could have asked for hospitality, they entered a temple which was called the "Capitol of Egypt". In this temple stood 365 idols, to which on appointed days divine honour was paid in idolatrous rites . . . But it came to pass that, when blessed Mary entered the temple with the child, all the idols fell to the ground, so that they all lay on their faces completely overturned and shattered. Thus they openly showed that they were nothings.

Here follows a quotation from Isa. 19:1, and the story continues:

When this was told to Affrodosius, the governor of that city, he came to the temple with his whole army . . . When he entered the temple and saw all the idols lying prostrate on their faces, he went up to the blessed Mary, who was carrying the Lord in her bosom and, worshipping him, said to his whole army and to all his friends: "If he were not the God of our gods, our gods would not have fallen on their faces before him, and they would not lie prostrate in his presence. Thus they silently confess him as their Lord. And if we do not with prudence do all that we see our gods do, we shall perhaps be in danger of angering him and of being destroyed, as happened to Pharaoh, king of the Egyptians, who was drowned in the sea with his whole army, because he did not believe such great wonders." Then all the people of the city believed in the Lord God through Jesus Christ.

The episode had often been the subject of painters; but they depict more the Christ after Constantine than the Christ of Matthew. Nearer to the biblical intention is the scene where, at the gate of an Egyptian city, Jesus and his parents are received by a woman who bows down in reverence. Sometimes an inscription identifies this woman as "Egyptica", the symbolic representative of Egypt, the land of refuge. A Byzantine miniature and a modern Egyptian painting (Plates 26 a and b) picture this warm welcome offered to Jesus in Egypt.

Too often readers of the Bible see Egypt as the "house of slavery", the land from whose tyranny the tribes of Israel had to be rescued. This narrows down the universal sovereignty of God and also limits the role of Egypt.

In a radical prophetic critique of the people of Israel, Amos saw in a vision God himself destroying the temple of Jerusalem and judging his people. He then heard God interrogating his covenant partner:

Are not you Israelites like Cushites
(Nubians or Ethiopians) to me? says the Lord.
Did I not bring Israel up from Egypt,
the Philistines from Caphtor (Crete),
the Aramaeans from Kir (Mesopotamia)? (Am. 9:7)

The decisive liberation story for the people of Israel, the Exodus, is here put side by side with other liberation

Plates 26(a) and (b): "Welcome to Egypt"
a) Byzantine miniature, 11th century.
b) Modern Egyptian painting by Little Sisters of Jesus, contemporary.

stories of other people, in which God is equally involved. The covenant people are chosen for a task, not for special privileges. Whether Israelite tribes are freed from an oppressive Pharaoh in Egypt or Palestinians from an oppressive government in the state of Israel, God's Word proclaims good news for the victims, and for the oppressors it is always a call to conversion—or judgment.

In all these liberation stories Egypt does not often play the role of the oppressor. On the contrary, in several biblical passages it is seen as the classic land of refuge. After Jacob and his sons had been rescued by Joseph, with the consent of the Pharaoh, from a famine (compare above p. 79), other Israelites found refuge in Egypt: when Jeroboam, the later king of the ten Northern tribes of Israel, rebelled against Solomon and was in danger, "he fled to king Shishak in Egypt and remained there till Solomon's death" (1 Kings 11:40). Similarly, when prophet Uriah prophesied against Jerusalem, so that king Jehoiakim sought to put him to death, Uriah "fled to Egypt" though later he would nevertheless be killed (Jer. 26:21ff). Even Jeremiah was forced to seek refuge in Egypt (Jer. 43f). Despite his prophecies of doom, for many centuries a Jewish colony flourished in that land where they had made their home.

The figure of the welcoming Egyptica in Plate 26 reminds us of this often forgotten role of Egypt. The Coptic Christians in Egypt, however, have not forgotten this. The places where, according to ancient traditions, Jesus and his parents received welcome and rest are still well-known. Across the many centuries they provide to believers an intimate link with Jesus. This is beautifully expressed in the following prayer by Marie Assaad, a Coptic Christian:

My Egyptian heart longs, O my God, for the redemption of my people. It has been our shame that the oppression of the Pharaohs drove the children of Israel to the sea. But you, my God, who free us from all our sins, you who make all things new, chose this same country as a shelter for the Holy Family, and a home to that One who was persecuted and oppressed that we might have life and have it abundantly.

Thank you, my Saviour, for the greatest gift you have given me. As a little girl my heart bubbled with joy every time I was taken to play under the tree in Matariah where you rested with Mary, your mother, and Joseph. I loved to touch the stone upon which your crib was placed in that dark underground church in old Cairo. I felt your presence. I heard your cry and laughter. I wept with the mothers whose children were killed by Herod. I rejoiced over your safety. I praised and continue to praise you, my Saviour and Redeemer, who take us out of the darkness into your marvellous light.

Out of Egypt

4:19 God to Moses: "Go
back to Egypt, for all
those who wished to
kill you are dead."

2:20 God to Joseph: "Go
to the land of Israel
for the men who
threatened the child's
life are dead."

In the Greek translation of the Old Testament and the original Greek version of the New Testament exactly the same verbs and expressions are often used, which suggests that these cannot be accidental similarities. Moreover, by the time of Matthew the Jewish historian Josephus was writing in his *Antiquities* details about the infancy of Moses which provided even more striking parallels to Matthew's infancy narratives of Jesus.

According to Josephus's account, in Egypt "one of the sacred scribes—persons with considerable skill in accurately predicting the future—announced to the king that there would be born to the Israelites at that time one who would abase the sovereignty of the Egyptians and exalt the Israelites, were he reared to manhood. He would surpass all men in virtue and win everlasting renown." Pharaoh ordered therefore all the new-born Hebrew boys to be cast into the Nile. Alarmed by this, the father of Moses, Amran, prayed to God that his son might be spared. Then—according to Josephus' account—he received, like Jesus' father, a divine message in a dream: "God had compassion on him and, moved by his supplication, appeared to him in his sleep, exhorting him not to despair of the future . . ." For this child "shall escape those who are watching to destroy him and, reared in a marvellous wise, he shall deliver the Hebrew race from their bondage in Egypt, and be remembered, so long as the universe shall endure, not by Hebrews alone but even by alien nations."

It is strange that Matthew ends the passage of the flight *to* Egypt with the quotation referring to the Exodus: "I call my son *out of* Egypt" (Hos. 11:1; Mt. 2:15).

One would expect this quotation to be part of the story after Joseph's third dream leading to the return from Egypt (Mt. 2:19–23). However, this scene of the return is wholly centred on the aim of the journey: the Lord's angel directs Joseph in his third dream "to the land of Israel", generally the whole of Palestine. Yet during the journey to Bethlehem where, according to Matthew, Joseph and Mary presumably had their home, Joseph receives in a fourth dream a more precise direction: "to the region of Galilee". Finally the actual place for their provisional settlement in Galilee is mentioned: Nazareth. This village from which Jesus' ministry starts (Mt. 4:13) is alluded to in a puzzling quotation from the prophets: "He shall be called a Nazarene." Besides evoking the name of Nazareth the term "Nazarene" probably designates Jesus also as a *nazir*, one set apart for God's service like Samson, Samuel and John the baptist, and as the *neser*, the messianic branch growing out of the stock of Jesse (Isa. 11:1).

The story of the flight *to* Egypt ends in Matthew's Gospel with a quotation about the call *out of* Egypt because of the parallels between the infancy narratives of Moses and of Jesus. The portrayal of Jesus as a new Moses and the suggestion that Jesus in his childhood recapitulates essential parts of the history of Israel are indeed characteristic traits of the whole of the Gospel (compare above pp. 63ff). The following parallels can, for instance, be detected:

Exodus	*Matthew*
1:10 The Pharaoh is afraid of increasing Israelite population.	2:3 Herod is afraid of the new-born messianic King.
1:16, 22 Pharaoh orders the killing of Hebrew boys.	2:8, 16 Herod plans to kill Jesus, orders a massacre in Bethlehem.
2:3, 9, 15 Moses is hid, rescued, and escapes.	2:13, 15 Jesus escapes and is rescued.
2:23 Pharaoh dies.	2:19 Herod dies.

The flight to Egypt, the massacre of the children in Bethlehem, and the return of Joseph with Jesus and Mary to Palestine—all these may well have happened as they are told. They are in keeping with what we know about the ageing Herod and the upheavals in Judaea after his death. It is strange, however, that none of the other evangelists reports these striking events and even Matthew never refers back to them. Whether these stories transmit factual history or not, their significance and purpose in Matthew's teaching are clear: the infant Jesus recapitulates the history of the people of Israel.

To capture this in a visual presentation one would have to make a composite image with the patriarch Joseph and the infant Moses in the background, the threatening Pharaoh and the angry Herod on both sides and a refugee family in the midst.

Throughout the centuries Christian iconography has mainly concentrated on the central group of the refugee family. Plate 27 shows how the contemporary Japanese artist Sadao Watanabe sees this significant episode in Jesus' early life. It is no more the triumphal departure of the one born to be king who begins to claim the whole of creation, as the scene is often portrayed in ancient Christian and medieval art. The mood in Watanabe's print is one of uncertainty—apprehensive parents sheltering the vulnerable child, moving on from danger to a still uncertain future. Prints of Watanabe on this and other scenes of Jesus' life can be found on calendars in many Japanese homes and restaurants. That is how the artist wants it to be: a public testimony, strongly influenced by the ancient Japanese popular art, showing Jesus in the midst of everyday life as the one who serves and suffers.

Another great interpreter of biblical faith in modern Japan is the widely read novelist Shusaku Endo. As a personal testimony he wrote his book, *A Life of Jesus*, where the Immanuel is shown as the one who "suffers with us". Endo does not include the childhood narratives in his account, but throughout his testimony the vulnerability of the Immanuel is emphasized. The chapter entitled "Jesus the ineffectual" shows how the teacher and healer from Nazareth was gradually rejected because he responded to a deeper need of the poor and the despised ones: "What they needed more than miraculous cures was love. Jesus knew the longing of human beings for changeless, enduring companionship. They needed a companion, the kind of a mother who could share their wretched suffering and weep together with them. He believed that God by his nature was not in the image of a stern father, but was more like a mother who shares the suffering of her children and weeps with them; and in order to bear witness to the love which God bore for these men and women in their misfortunes, whenever Jesus met them near the Lake of Galilee he prayed that in God's kingdom they would arrive at his way of seeing things: Blessed are the poor in spirit, for theirs is the kingdom of heaven."

This beatitude is like a *cantus firmus* in Endo's book. In the chapter on Christ's passion he writes: "An enormous contrast is evident between Jesus during the passion and Jesus before the passion. One side is Jesus the powerful, the other is Jesus the powerless. The evangelists did not hesitate in their narratives of the passion to write about Jesus being powerless, about Jesus helpless, with love alone continuing to flow from within him, about Jesus worn out, about Jesus exhausted. The quintessence of what Jesus taught us comes home to me (speaking for myself) not so much from that dynamic Jesus in Galilee as from this helpless Jesus on the cross."

In Watanabe's print we see the helpless Jesus not yet on the cross, but as a vulnerable infant. He thus became the companion of all who suffer a similar fate.

Plate 27: *"Flight to Egypt", colour print by Sadao Watanabe, Japan. 1979.*

Sadao Watanabe 1999

Refugees

When the Ugandan artist Francis Sekitoleko was asked to contribute to this volume, he painted an everyday scene in Uganda today (Plate 28): an African family on the move, having gathered the few possessions which remained after the horrors of war and pillage. The mother, the father and one child have survived, but only for the time; armed robbers may be waiting round the corner. They will take away what little these refugees have and they may even kill them.

This is the manner in which millions of refugees in Africa and Asia, the Near East, Central and South America interpret today the flight to Egypt. It is an existential interpretation, needing no theological explanations, nor any complicated hermeneutics in order to make the link between the biblical story and their own life's story. They understand with their tired feet, their threatened existence and their flickering hope.

An African poet, Albert Abble, looked out for a black virgin:

I'm looking for an African painter
who will make me a black Virgin,
a Virgin with a fine "keowa"
like our mothers wear . . .
Isn't it true, Mother, that you
are the Mother of the Blacks too,
a black Mother, carrying the infant Jesus on her back?

In Sekitoleko's painting we see the black Mother. Yet there remains a fundamental difference between the poem and the painting. The Catholic poet sees Mary's quality of being the mother of all through her triumphant assumption into heaven, a doctrine that came later, and has no biblical basis:

Since your Assumption,
since the glorious day
when you were triumphantly
carried away into heaven,
you no longer have any colour.
Or rather, you are all colours.

Sekitoleko, in contrast, sees the universality of Mary, Joseph and Jesus in their sharing the human condition with all its uncertainties and sufferings.

The point where all colours and cultures converge is where God becomes a vulnerable human being, the Immanuel as a refugee.

When later Jesus taught in Galilee a learned scribe came up to him and said: "Master, I will follow you wherever you go." Jesus then said—and he who in early childhood already had been a refugee and later a displaced person had indeed every reason to say so: "Foxes have their holes, the birds have their roosts; but the Son of Man has nowhere to lay his head" (Mt. 8:19f). For those well established in life, this is a tremendous challenge. When subsequently a rich man was faced with this radical demand of discipleship and could not respond to it, the disciples rightly asked whether such a vulnerable life to which Jesus calls us was at all possible. "Jesus looked at them and said: 'For human people it is impossible; but everything is possible for God'" (Mt. 19:24ff).

Discipleship remains a miracle, a human impossibility, for rich and poor, strong and weak, for people well settled with all their possessions and for refugees on an uncertain road. Yet the poor and the weak and the refugees can more easily recognize the Immanuel. He chose to be one among them and he addressed to them a very special invitation:

Come to me, all whose work is hard,
whose load is heavy;
and I will give you relief.
Bend your necks to my yoke,
and learn from me,
for I am gentle and humble-hearted;
and your souls will find relief.
For my yoke is good to bear,
my load is light (Mt. 11:28ff).

The Immanuel as a refugee. This understanding of the flight to Egypt speaks most strongly to people in our times. It is neither the "flight" as a triumphal, imperial going out for conquest (compare above p. 82), nor its Old Testament background with parallels to the patriarch Joseph, to Jacob/Israel and the infancy narratives of Moses (compare above pp. 79ff and 85ff) that gives Matthew's account its poignant relevance for today. It is the Immanuel recognized as a refugee heading towards darkening skies, as Sekitoleko shows him in his painting.

The Immanuel coming as a suffering prophet, as the totally unexpected *suffering* Messiah: this is the scandal and the good news of Matthew's teaching. He cares very especially for "the little ones", for the "least", as Matthew does not tire of insisting:
—"If anyone gives so much as a cup of cold water to one of these little ones, because he is a disciple of mine, I tell you this: that one will assuredly not go unrewarded" (Mt. 10:42).

Plate 28: *"Flight to Egypt", oil painting by Francis Sekitoleko, Uganda. 1980.*

—"Whoever receives one such child in my name receives me. But if anyone is a cause of stumbling to one of these little ones who have faith in me, it would be better for him to have a millstone hung round his neck and be drowned in the depth of the sea" (Mt. 18:5f).
—"It is not your heavenly Father's will that one of these little ones should be lost" (Mt. 18:14).
—"I tell you this: anything you did for one of my brothers here, however humble, you did for me" (Mt. 25:40, 45).

The Immanuel as a refugee speaks to today's political emigrants. In their flight from military dictatorship, only now and then dare they stop and "briefly search . . . for the face of the one who said he was the light of the world". In a long poem, a deep *cri du coeur* (cry out of the heart) the Mexican writer Raúl Macín thus interprets the destiny of Latin American political refugees. Whether they know it or not, from his early childhood onwards Jesus is with these abused people on the move:

It was the dawn of a day in which hope
transformed all.
It was the dawn of the day in which victory
was not only felt
but rather was there, close by,
within reach of a people
who had not ceased to struggle for it.
It was the dawn of the dawning of a nation
when the boots of betrayal
began their destructive task.

And it was then when the night
of anguish
forced those who lived with hope
to seek refuge in a tenebrous exile.
And thus began a pilgrimage
that seems to have no end
in spite of its limits being rage
and nostalgia . . .

Step by step
amid remembrances, curses and dreams
leaving behind the night of torture,
the ignominy and the defeat
the people of latin american pilgrimage
seek refuge
in the conviction of returning.
Step by step,
at times with exasperating slowness
the pilgrims advance
in spite of the darkness of injustice.
Step by step
and only stopping briefly to search anxiously
as he who sees the invisible
for the face of the one who said
he was the light of the world.
Step by step
rebuilding hope
step by step
inventing faith
step by step
dreaming of victory . . .

My Son

Caught in the spider's web of life. So I sometimes see young mothers with their starving child, sitting somewhere in Georgetown. No husband. Abandoned. Almost undistinguishable from the background. It is as if the mother wished to take back her newly born child into the safety of her womb, as if the famished infant could breathe only from its mother's breath. For there is no room in our hard world for the little ones.

With such words the Guyanese artist Philip Alfonso Moore spoke about what had led him to create the painting reproduced in Plate 29.

Moore's picture of the flight to Egypt does not deal with the actual story, but rather interprets what happened in God's heart when he sent Jesus among us as the Immanuel. In his narrative of the flight, Matthew quotes from the eleventh chapter of the prophet Hosea. He does so because the beginning of this chapter refers to the Exodus and because he once more wants to emphasize that the infant Jesus recapitulates that crucial period of Israelite history. By quoting the beginning of a story, psalm or prophetic oracle, Jewish teachers often implicitly refer to the whole passage. This may have been the intention of Matthew when he quoted Hosea 11:1, for what follows reveals, better than any other passage in the Old Testament, the nature of the God who became the Immanuel in Jesus.

When Israel was a boy, I loved him;
I called my son out of Egypt (Hos. 11:1).

The "boy" here is not Jesus, but the people of Israel. Instead of responding to such love, they alienated themselves from their God who, according to Hosea, is full of motherly care:

The more I called, the further they went from me.

It was I who taught Ephraim to walk,
I who had taken them in my arms;
but they did not know that I harnessed them
in leading-strings
and led them with bonds of love—
that I had lifted them like a little child to my cheek,
that I had bent down to feed them (vss 2–4).

The infidelity of the beloved people stirs the anger of God:

Back they shall go to Egypt,
the Assyrian shall be their king;
for they have refused to return to me.
The sword shall be swung . . .
bent on rebellion as they are (vss 5ff).

Then an unheard-of thing happens: God repents. God cannot but be God. He must forgive; he must continue to love and cherish.

How can I give up, Ephraim,
how surrender you, Israel?

My heart is changed within me,
my remorse kindles already.
I will not let loose my fury,
I will not turn round and destroy Ephraim;
for I am God and not man,
the Holy One in your midst (vss 8f).

Matthew applied the beginning of Hosea's prophecy to Jesus. For him God's Son had become incarnate not in a people, but in a person. Immediately after the infancy narratives he reports about the baptism of Jesus where the Immanuel is annointed before the eyes of John the baptist by the Spirit of God. Contrary to the account given by Mark, Matthew gives us to understand that the divine acknowledgment by the voice from heaven was heard publicly, not only by Jesus. This Son of God was now going to make public and effective God's repentance through his ministry, death and resurrection. What according to the eleventh chapter of Hosea had happened in the heart of God was now becoming God's incarnate love in his Son.

The lonely woman in Philip A. Moore's painting depicts not only Mary during the flight to Egypt, but it points also to that God full of motherly care, the amazing God who decides to repent of his anger, as Hosea prophesied. This is the God who came among us in the Immanuel, in that famished infant of Moore's painting, threatened by the Herods of all times (Plate 29).

While the artist worked on this painting the words of a song came to him which he entitled "No room". It speaks about the fact that there was no room for the Immanuel when he came into this world. It recalls Herod's order to kill all the children, so that Jesus' family had to flee to Egypt. As in the painting, so also in this song the biblical scene is transposed into the harsh reality of the Caribbean region and of Central America. In prophetic protest he cries out: "I say it's wrong, to strangle young ones, that will have to fight when wars are on." Yet the poem also reminds us of Hosea's prophecy, that God will call out of Egypt his son, and of Jesus' word: "Thus suffer small ones to come to me!" The song thus challenges the present reality of sorrow: "The truth will conquer, come what may!"

The paradox of the incarnation, the Holy One among us in this vulnerable child, brings hope for those in whom human hopes are broken a thousand times. Such a "nevertheless" is sung in "Todos los dias nace el Señor", a Venezuelan carol by Juan Antonio Espinosa:

Into a world without light, Jesus Christ is born.
Coming to conquer the darkness, Jesus Christ is born.
He comes to bring us a new world,
: ‖ : Jesus our Lord is born every day! : ‖ :

Freedom is coming to all, Jesus Christ is born.
Chains of oppression are breaking, Jesus Christ is born.
Liberating all of God's children
: ‖ : Jesus our Lord is born every day! : ‖ :

Justice is coming to all, Jesus Christ is born.
There will be no more oppression, Jesus Christ is born.
He hears the cry of his people,
: ‖ : Jesus our Lord is born every day! : ‖ :

He is the friend of the poor, Jesus Christ is born.
He brings hope to all who suffer, Jesus Christ is born.
Earth's fruits are for all who labour
: ‖ : Jesus our Lord is born every day! : ‖ :

He comes to bring us his peace, Jesus Christ is born.
Where there is strife, blood, and hatred, Jesus Christ is born.
Wherever people are struggling,
: ‖ : Jesus our Lord is born every day! : ‖ :

He comes to teach us to love, Jesus Christ is born.
Throw off the shackles of hatred, Jesus Christ is born.
Join hands sisters and brothers!
: ‖ : Jesus our Lord is born every day! : ‖ :

He wakes the world from its sleep. Jesus Christ is born.
He stirs and calls us to action. Jesus Christ is born.
In every heart that is hopeful,
: ‖ : Jesus our Lord is born every day! : ‖ :

Plate 29: "No Room", painting by Philip A. Moore, Guyana. Contemporary.

John's vision

¹ In the beginning was the Logos,
  the Logos was in God's presence,
  and the Logos was God.
² He was present with God in the beginning.

³ Through him all things came into being,
  and apart from him not a thing came to be.
⁴ That which had come to be in him was life,
  and this life was the light of humankind.
⁵ The light shines on in the darkness,
  for the darkness did not overcome it.

(⁶There was sent by God a man named John ⁷who came as a witness to testify to the light so that through him everyone might believe—⁸but only to testify to the light, for he himself was not the light.)

⁹The real light
  which gives light to every human being
  was coming into the world!
¹⁰ He was in the world,
  and the world was made by him;
  yet the world did not recognize him.
¹¹ To his own he came;
  yet his own people did not accept him.
¹² But all those who did accept him
  he empowered to become God's children.

That is, those who believe in his name—¹³those who were begotten, not by blood, nor by carnal desire, nor by man's desire, but by God.

¹⁴ And the Logos became flesh
  and pitched his tent among us.
  And we have seen his glory,
  the glory of an only Son coming from the Father,
  filled with grace and truth.
(¹⁵John testified to him by proclaiming: "This is he of whom I said, 'The one who comes after me ranks ahead of me, for he existed before me.'")
¹⁶ And of his fullness
  we have all had a share—
  grace in place of grace.
¹⁷For while the Law was a gift through Moses, this grace and truth came through Jesus Christ. ¹⁸No one has ever seen God; it is God the only Son, ever at the Father's side, who has revealed Him.

John 1:1–18

The above translation is adapted from Raymond E. Brown's Commentary on John.

the new baptism—baptism of water and of the Spirit;
the new Passover—his flesh and his blood
given for the life of the world.
He is the nourishing Bread,
the thirst-quenching Water, the life-giving Wine,
Heavenly liturgy, made incarnate,
Transfigured matter, infused with life by the Spirit,
An earnest of eternity.

In these words, one who deeply meditated on the Fourth Gospel, Suzanne de Dietrich, has caught John's vision.

While John writes as Rembrandt paints, to read his Gospel is like looking at a Chinese print. In the foreground we see everyday scenes drawn with much greater detail than in the other Gospels: a marriage feast in the Galilean village of Cana, a Samaritan woman at the well, a home in Bethany near Jerusalem where two bereaved sisters mourn for their brother. Everything is clearly visible, realistically drawn. Behind such everyday scenes Chinese prints often show trees and mountains, as it were through a haze, further away. And as we look more carefully, still another layer of reality appears, a horizon vaguely visible where heaven and earth meet. Similarly John's highly evocative language lets us discover behind Jesus' earthly life ever new layers of meaning. His Gospel can never be fully comprehended. In it always there are new discoveries to be made.

In principio erat verbum—"In the beginning was the Word": this very first sentence of John's prologue forms the first page of the Fourth Gospel in the Book of Kells (Plate 30). The intricate Irish calligraphy with its complex ornamentation almost hides the text and even the evangelist who came to witness.

Ever since the prologue and the Gospel were written theologians have wondered who this witness was and what he really wanted to say. Reading some of the recent Johannine studies in various languages one feels as lost in the labyrinth of hypotheses as one would be lost in the tortuously winding strings of the Irish miniature.

Papias, the bishop of Hieropolis (ca. A.D. 140), makes a distinction between the apostle John and an elder John. It was Irenaeus, the bishop of Lyons (ca. 180–200), who first claimed that "John, the disciple of the Lord who had reclined on his bosom", published the Gospel in Ephesus. More than a century later the church historian Eusebius wrote that "John, who had employed all his time in proclaiming the gospel orally, finally proceeded to write". He was asked to do so in order to complete the three other Gospels, because "there was lacking in them an account of the deeds done by Christ at the beginning of his ministry".

The Gospel itself never mentions John the Zebedee by name, nor does it clearly identify "the beloved disciple" with the apostle John. Nevertheless, the eye-witness mentioned in the Gospel (Jn 1:14; 19:35) can indeed

With the first sentences of his Gospel John takes us on a vertiginous flight. He brings us to the beginning of everything, the time even before creation. He lifts us up into the transcendent sphere of God. He thus gives us a perspective which embraces all things and all nations, the whole cosmos. No wonder the eagle became the symbol of this evangelist.

In this infinite time and space there is a centre, a force which creates, brings the crisis of separation and knits together what participates in the true life: the Logos, the "Word" of God. John testifies that this Logos has become incarnate, has become flesh, in Jesus Christ.

John writes like Rembrandt paints:

All is contrast of shadow and light.
Jesus is in the centre, standing in an orb of light.
All the faces turned towards him are lighted up.
Those who turn from him are in darkness.
Believing in the Son is passing
from darkness to light, from death to life.
That is why all is submitted to him,
Just as he is altogether submitted to his Father.
He is the divine Word made flesh.
His work is to establish the new form of worship,
in spirit and in truth:
the new temple—his body;

have been John the Zebedee. This does not necessarily make him the evangelist. He might simply have started the *oral* Johannine tradition and acted as the main source of information. This would account for the fact that the Fourth Gospel in places contains more accurate historic information than the earlier Gospels, although the text was probably given its present form only in the last decade of the 1st century.

John's Gospel clearly had behind it a long history of oral tradition, as Eusebius rightly states. Even after the eye-witness, or a perceptive disciple of his, had put down the testimony in writing, further editorial work like the addition of chapter 21 was completed by later editors. Moreover, some time in this process of oral and written transmission a shift from the original Judaean setting to the religious milieu in Asia Minor occurred. Thus the language and thought patterns of the Gospel have certain similarities with the Jewish inter-testamental literature, especially the teachings of the Community of Qumran in the Judaean desert, and hellenistic Judaism and popular philosophies in Asia Minor.

Such a shift from one cultural and religious setting to another accounts for many of the puzzles we face when carefully reading the Gospel. There are for instance two different and seemingly contradictory major emphases in John's vision of what happened in Jesus Christ. They are already evident in the prologue.

On the one hand, the accent clearly is on the fact that Jesus comes from the heavenly Father and returns to him. He is the unique Son of God who reveals and accomplishes the Father's love and will. The other Gospels contain three announcements of Jesus' future suffering and death. John, however, writes about three announcements of Jesus' elevation. The passion story is narrated with this emphasis: no struggle in prayer in Gethsemane; Jesus himself carries the cross and leads the way; no cry of god-forsakenness. Jesus is aware of God's plan and retains the initiative until the end, when by the giving of himself he accomplishes the Father's love and will. The crucifixion is thus the elevation, the beginning of the return to the Father.

In line with this first main emphasis is the fact that, unlike in the other three Gospels, there is in John no account of the transfiguration. This most "Johannine" event in Jesus' life is for John much more than one among many events. He reinterprets the whole tradition about Jesus in the light of the transfiguration, indeed as one great transfiguration story.

The other major emphasis is that on the incarnation of the Logos. The "Word" became flesh. In Eastern iconography, which is strongly influenced by John's Gospel, the fact of the real birth is emphasized by the scene with the bathing of the new-born infant (compare the icon of nativity, Plate 14). The bread from heaven can and must be eaten: "Whoever eats my flesh and drinks my blood possesses eternal life" (Jn 6:54). The

most "spiritual" among the Gospels is also the most "material". If Mark's Gospel faces us more clearly than any other with the scandalous paradox of the cross, John's Gospel emphasizes the almost unbelievable paradox of the incarnation. How can he who is so altogether at one with the heavenly Father become so utterly human?

John's prologue forms a different type of overture to the "symphony" of his Gospel from Luke's and Matthew's infancy narratives or Mark's prologue. In the first place, it is clearly a mixture of poetry and prose. This has led many biblical scholars to assume that the evangelist used, edited and expanded a hymn to the Logos which used to be sung in the churches for which John wrote.

This assumption could explain why some of the key terms of the prologue no longer appear in the Gospel itself—for example the leading term "Logos", "God's Word". One might rightly object that after his incarnation this Logos bears a name: "Jesus". (John mentions this name in fact much more often than any other evangelist.) But the terms "fullness", "grace", and the verb "to pitch a tent" are also not taken up later. Further, the prologue does not explicitly mention the cross and the resurrection of Jesus.

Nevertheless, these unique features of the prologue are far outweighed by its many anticipations of later gospel terms and themes. The following is by no means a complete list:

Jn 1:1	since before the world	Jn 17:5
Jn 1:4, 9	light of the world	Jn 8:12; 9:5
Jn 1:5	opposition light/darkness	Jn 3:19
Jn 1:14	seeing his glory	Jn 12:41
Jn 1:14	the only Son	Jn 3:16
Jn 1:18	only the Son saw the Father	Jn 6:46
Jn 1:6, 15	John the baptist	Jn 1:19, 30

Some see in verses 11 and 12 an anticipation of the first and second part of John's Gospel, which commentaries often call the Book of Signs (chapters 1–12), and the Book of Glory (chapters 13–20).

No agreement has been reached as to where the poetry ends and the prose begins, or as to what belongs to the Johannine hymn and what to the evangelist's annotations. Some therefore reject the hypothesis of an early hymn altogether and ascribe the whole prologue to John. The separation between hymn and annotations, proposed in the translation on page 95 is merely a well informed guess. Clearly the passages on John the baptist (vss 6–8 and vs 15) did not belong to an original hymn. These verses might originally have formed, together with John 1:19ff, the beginning

Plate 30: "In principio erat verbum". Title page of John's Gospel in the Book of Kells, Ireland. Second half of 8th or early 9th century.

of the Gospel. They were probably inserted into the hymn in order to root the coming of the Logos firmly in human history.

Possible explanatory notes to the preceding lines of the hymn may be the end of verse 12 and the whole of verse 13 (some consider also verses 2, 9 and 16 as such notes, while others believe that the original hymn ended already with verse 12). The two closing verses of the prologue are sometimes attributed to the hymn, but more likely they were written with a definite purpose in mind: in verse 17 the evangelist situates the incarnation within the history of salvation, and in verse 18 he emphasizes once again the union of the Son with the Father as well as the Son's revealing function.

For understanding the message of the prologue another question going beyond its literary form is crucial: Where does the earthly ministry of Jesus begin? Some see the whole prologue as a hymn to the incarnate Logos. More likely, the evangelist first wants to lead us beyond all earthly space and time, giving us a glimpse of that perfect union, where the Logos is totally turned towards God (vss 1–2). Then only does the Logos turn to his work of creation, to all things and all human beings (vss 3–5). But when does the Logos become incarnate in Jesus? Is this the case already from verse 3 onwards? Probably those are right who see Jesus' earthly ministry beginning either from verses 9 and 10 or only from verse 14 onwards. These two possibilities will be explored in the following biblical reflections.

Such detailed analyses of form and content must not prevent us from feeling the force and beauty of the first eighteen verses of John's Gospel. For centuries the prologue was recited as the final prayer and blessing in the Roman mass. It is indeed a passage to be learned by heart, to be recited and pondered over. The sound of John's prologue must be heard and its imagery imprint itself on our minds.

The invincible light

In the beginning of creation, when God made heaven and earth, the earth was without form and void, with darkness over the face of the abyss . . . God said, "Let there be light", and there was light; and God saw that the light was good, and he separated light from darkness (Gen. 1:1–4).

In his prologue John clearly refers back to that first beginning in the Book of Genesis. He leads us even beyond the act of creation to God's transcendent being. Unlike in much religious writing of the time of John, we are not given a description of heaven or speculations about God living alone. The only affirmation made is that of perfect union between the Logos and God. The Logos is turned towards God and living in God's presence.

Then the first of many shifts in John's prologue occurs: the Logos turns outward, begins his creative activity, calling into being the whole creation, life and light:

Through him all things came into being,
and apart from him not a thing came to be.
That which had come to be in him was life,
and this life was the light of humankind.
The light shines on in the darkness,
for the darkness did not overcome it.

Who is this Logos? Jesus never applied this expression to himself. Only in three passages in the whole New Testament is he called the Logos, all in Johannine writings (Jn 1:1, 14; 1 Jn 1:1; Rev. 19:13). In the Jewish and Greek religious philosophies of the centuries before and after Christ the term Logos played a very important role. Philo, the Jewish philosopher of Alexandria and a contemporary of Jesus, often wrote about the Logos as the intermediary between God and the creatures. Itinerant Stoic philosophers preached the Logos as the moving divine Reason which they taught to be immanent in all things.

As a good interpreter of the gospel John might have used this term because it had such a wide resonance in the contemporary Jewish and Graeco-Roman world. However, the Logos had for him a thoroughly Semitic, Old-Testamental and inter-testamental meaning. The Hebrew term for God's Word is *dabar* which means both word and event. This *dabar* can both be heard and

seen, it acts in creation, judgment and healing. The Old Testament is full of examples for this, not only in the creation story, more often in fact in the books of the prophets and in the Psalms:

The Lord's Word made the heavens . . .
and all people on earth stand in awe of him.
For he spoke, and it was (Ps. 33:6ff).

With you is the fountain of life,
and in your light we are bathed with light (Ps. 36:9).

During and after the Babylonian exile, God was experienced as a far-away reality, unapproachable in holiness. Therefore God's Word was described almost as a person, as God's agent in the created world (compare Isa. 55:10–11 and similar passages in Isa. 40–66).

This tendency to see in God's Word almost a person went much farther with regard to God's Wisdom. Indeed, in the Old Testament and inter-testamental wisdom literature (compare above pp. 73ff) God's Wisdom was more and more seen as a personified manifestation of God, participating in God's work of creation and revelation. It is this personified Wisdom which most strongly influenced John's use of the term Logos. In the following texts from the Proverbs and the inter-testamental book of Wisdom of Solomon (ca. 100 B.C.) one could often replace the Wisdom who speaks with the Logos of John's prologue:

The Lord created me the beginning of his works,
before all else that he made, long ago . . .
When he set the heavens in their place I was there . . .
I was at his side each day like a master workman
(other possible translation: "his little child, his delight"
Prov. 8:22ff).

Wisdom "is the brightness that streams from everlasting light,
the flawless mirror of the active power of God
and the image of his goodness.
She is but one, yet can do everything;
herself unchanging, she makes all things new;
age after age she enters into holy souls,
and makes them God's friends and prophets,
for nothing is acceptable to God but the man
who makes his home with wisdom.
She is more radiant than the sun,
and surpasses every constellation;
compared with the light of the day,
she is found to excel;
for day gives place to night,
but against wisdom no evil can prevail" (Wisd. 7:26–30).

For all affirmations in John 1:1–5 and 10–12 one could quote similar parallels from the Wisdom literature. In these verses the evangelist says nothing which believing Jews of his time could not have said for God's Word and Wisdom. Yet he associates the Logos, who became incarnate in Jesus, with all these effective words of God and with the international Wisdom of the sages.

No Christmas feast was celebrated during the first three centuries of the Christian era. The church confessed above all the crucified and risen Lord. Every Sunday, the day of resurrection, was thus *the* Christian feast, with the annual observance of the Passion and Easter celebrations soon added to it.

We saw how, in the course of the Christian reflection about Jesus, the moment of his becoming the Son of God was gradually dated backwards: from his resurrection in the earliest creeds to his baptism in Mark's witness, from there to his conception according to the infancy narratives in the Gospels of Luke and Matthew, and from there to the beginning of time when the Logos was turned towards God, in John's prologue (compare above pp. 32–4). A similar movement backwards can be observed in the church's liturgical feasts.

In the course of the 2nd century, disciples of the Gnostic teacher Basilides began in Alexandria to celebrate Jesus' baptism as his manifestation (*epiphaneia*) on earth. They chose the 6th or 10th of January as a date, and it is likely that they did so in order to replace with this Christian feast other celebrations which were observed in early January: e.g., the birth of the Alexandrian god Eon and feasts for Dionysius and Osiris. From the early 4th century onwards Epiphany was celebrated in the whole Eastern church. During the night, 5th to 6th of January, Christians recalled Jesus' birth and on the 6th of January they celebrated his baptism, and later some of his miracles as well.

The star of the Magi and the light shining in the darkness played the central role during the nocturnal worship commemorating Christ's birth. The Syrian church father Ephraem (4th century) describes the great joy with which this celebration was observed in Christian homes and by the worshipping assembly. He wrote the following hymn for the feast of Epiphany:

The whole creation proclaims him,
To him the Magi bear witness,
the star also announces him:
See, here is the Son of the King!
The heavens are opened,
Jordan's waters foam,
The dove appears:
Behold, my Son, my Beloved.

The Western church soon adopted the feast of Epiphany, but within a short time the celebration of Jesus' birth was separated from his epiphany. The Christmas feast was fixed on the 25th of December. Why this sudden interest in a separate celebration of the incarnation? And why this change of date?

The answer to the first question is a theological one. In 325, the Council of Nicea had condemned as heresy the belief that at the birth of Jesus, not God but only a heavenly being had become a human person. The Council also rejected the teaching that at his baptism Jesus was merely "adopted" as God's Son. It therefore became imperative to mark with a separate liturgical feast the true faith in the real incarnation of God in Jesus.

Nothing can be known from the Bible about the day of either Jesus' baptism or birth. On the day of the solstice, 25th of December, great festivities for the sun used to be held. The members of the Persian Mithras cult which, since the 3rd century A.D., had a strong influence in the Roman army, devoted that day for celebration in honour of their god of light. Yet even before the spread of the Mithras cult in the West, temples to the *sol invictus*, the undefeated and invincible sun, had been erected in Rome. Therefore the emperor Constantine—half Christian, half sun-worshipper—planned to combine the feast of the sun with the birth of Christ. In A.D. 321 he already had introduced the sunday as an official weekly day of rest. The Western church was keenly interested to shift the feast of Christ's birth from Epiphany to 25th of December, for it thus hoped to replace pre-Christian festivities with a true worship of the God incarnate in Jesus Christ.

The first Christmas celebration on the 25th of December in Rome is attested for the year 336. Gradually the Eastern Church also accepted this separate feast and its date, since 379 in Constantinople, in Syria since 386, in Egypt only since 431. The Armenian Orthodox Church, however, celebrates until today Christ's birth on the feast of Epiphany.

Before all this happened an unknown Christian artist created that daring visible confession of faith found in an ancient Christian cemetery under the present St Peter's basilica in Rome reproduced in Plate 31. Was he a former member of the Mithras cult who was now drawn towards the light of Christ, brighter than that of the Persian god of light? He certainly knew and perhaps had participated in the Roman festivities in honour of the *sol invictus* on the 25th of December. In his mosaic he shows Christ as the sun with the sun-wagon, amidst tendrils of vine, symbols both of life and the life-giving eucharist.

It is not the incarnate Jesus but the Logos before incarnation in the first part of John's prologue whom we meet in this early Christian visual confession. He is the same as the risen Christ, the Lord of the whole universe, the light of all human beings.

Plate 31: *Christ as* sol invictus, *early Christian mosaic, Necropolis under St Peter, Rome. 3rd or early 4th century.*

The light of humankind

Long before Jesus' birth was celebrated in Rome as a feast of light, the great Alexandrian teacher Clemens wrote, around A.D. 200, a hymn to Christ, the light of humanity:

Now all became light which never fades,
The side of the sunset is transformed in its rising.
The new creation reveals its meaning.
For in the sun's wagon he rides through the universe,
the sun of righteousness,
without distinction he visits the whole of humanity.
He follows thus his Father who lets rise the sun
and drips the dew of truth on all human beings.

Does this hymn of Clemens say essentially what John's prologue reveals about the Logos who enlightens the whole of humankind (Jn 1:4, 9)? After the prologue John's Gospel concentrates on Jesus, the incarnate Logos. There it is made clear that true life, light and truth can only be gained in communion with him who said: "I am the way, the truth and the life; no one comes to the Father except by me" (Jn 14:6). Yet what about those who never received a true testimony about the incarnate Logos? Has the divine "dew of truth" not fallen on them? Did the light of all human beings discriminate against them?

Before giving his testimony about the incarnate Lord, the evangelist reminds us of the work of the Logos prior to his incarnation in Jesus. First there is the wide focus envisaging the creation and the life of the whole cosmos (verse 4a). The focus narrows down to the whole of humanity (vss 4b. 9–10), and the people of Israel (vs 11). The prologue follows the flow of the first biblical account of creation where only after the creation of the inanimate and the animate world God says, "Let us make the human being in our image and likeness . . .", and so "created the humankind in his own image, . . . male and female he created them . . . And God saw all that he had made, and it was very good/beautiful" (Gen. 1:26–31).

In medieval iconography there are remarkable miniatures, frescoes and sculptures which show not God the Father, but the Logos in this creating activity. He is portrayed stooping down with a pair of compasses to bring order into the chaos of the world, or already surrounded by the created animal world. One of the most moving visual interpretations of this creative art of the Logos is a series of sixteen sculptured reliefs on the northern porch of the cathedral of Chartres. Plate 32 shows the Logos envisaging the creation of the human being. It is not yet the act of creating itself, which appears on another relief in this series. Just as an artist sometimes inwardly sees the finished work while looking at the still empty canvas or the crude block of marble, so the Logos projects that being which is to become the image of God, enlightened by God's Word and Wisdom.

The real light
which gives light to every human being
was coming into the world!
He was in the world.
and the world was made by him;
yet the world did not recognize him.
To his own he came;
yet his own people did not accept him.
But all those who did accept him
he empowered to become God's children.

Do these verses of John's prologue already speak about the Logos incarnate in Jesus, about Jesus' earthly ministry? Or do they still refer to the Logos before incarnation who—like the personified Wisdom—participates in God's creating and revealing work? Good arguments for both understandings have been put forward, and both meet with special difficulties.

If this part of the prologue refers to Jesus' earthly ministry, one can understand why the evangelist put the testimony of John the baptist between verses 5 and 9. The probable annotation of the hymn in verses 12c and 13 identifies then "those who did accept him" and those who "become children of God" with Christian believers, who have been "born from water and spirit" (Jn 3:3–8). All that the prologue affirms in verses 9–12 will indeed also be said by Jesus or about Jesus, the incarnate Logos, in the course of John's Gospel. Yet does not this first understanding detract from the clear affirmation that the Logos enlightens the *whole* of humanity? And if here the evangelist already intends the incarnation, why is the explicit affirmation about the Logos becoming incarnate placed only in verse 14?

Should we not rather understand verses 9–12 in the prologue as still describing the work of the Logos before incarnation? He is present as light in the world of creation and in the midst of all human beings (vss 9–10). He is present also among the Israelites before and after the coming of the Christ (vs 11). According to verse 7 John the baptist came to witness so that *everyone* (not just the Jews of Jesus' time) might believe through him. He can thus be understood as the representative of all

Plate 32: *The Logos envisaging the human being. Sculptured relief, Cathedral of Chartres, France. 13th century.*

prophets in world history who have witnessed to the light of the Logos. According to this understanding verse 12 refers not only to Christian believers. All those "children of God" before and after the coming of the Christ, both Jews and Gentiles, are included here—all who knew the Creator of all things, who received God and sought enlightenment from the Logos even if they could not name his name. It was shown earlier how strongly John's prologue is influenced by the wisdom literature (compare above p. 101). There one finds the same concern for the whole of humanity, the same openness to wisdom received also by those who do not know the God of Abraham, Isaac and Jacob.

However, is this second way of understanding not contradicted by the annotations in verses 12c and 13? There the "children of God" are those "who believe in his name, those who were begotten by God himself". This is commonly interpreted as referring to the new birth of Christian believers "from water and spirit". But could it not also refer to the openness of human beings to the light of the Logos, though they do not recognize that light as Jesus and know the Logos by other names? In that case the strongly polemical verse 13 would refer to those who, simply because of their race and genealogy, consider themselves to be God's children. Later the incarnate Logos will declare: "No one can come to me unless he is drawn by the Father who sent me; and I will raise him up on the last day. It is written in the prophets: 'And they shall all be taught by God.'

Everyone who has listened to the Father and learned from him comes to me" (Jn 6:44f). Is it this, being drawn by the Father and learning from him, which constitutes faith? Are these as yet not "Christian" believers among Jews and Gentiles the "other sheep of mine not belonging to this fold" (Jn 10:16), whom Jesus seeks?

Perhaps these two interpretations of the verses 9–12 are not mutually exclusive. What are presumably annotations by the evangelist favour more the first understanding, while what is probably the original hymn proclaims rather the second message. As the prologue now stands, this passage (including verses 12c and 13) gradually leads up to the climax, the incarnation of the Logos in Jesus (vs 14). The focus steadily narrows down, from the whole of humanity to the people of Israel and from there to those who accept Jesus.

The world did not recognize him,
his own people did not accept him.

World history and the history of the people of Israel are full of such deafness to God's Word and blindness to God's Wisdom. And yet in all ages and cultures there are those who are drawn by God, who learn from the Logos.

Because of God's love for this world in darkness and for all the people groping for light, the incarnation of the Logos became a necessity. John now begins to tell the story of this costly love.

Incarnation

And the Logos became flesh.

God's Word and Wisdom become incarnate in a frail human being. This is the very opposite of much religious aspiration both in the old days and today. Then, as now, salvation is often sought in an *ex-carnation*. By an otherworldly spirituality we seek to escape the hard realities of this world. Through daydreaming or biochemical help we attempt to go beyond the dullness and pain of concrete human life. By means of an ecstasy we endeavour to break out from the bondage of bodily existence with our "soul" and "mind" (in the Greek philosophical, not the biblical meaning of these terms).

Yet the Logos became *flesh*. The author of the hymn and the evangelist John could easily have chosen a less shocking term, for instance "human being" (in Greek: *anthropos*) or "man" (*anēr*). Deliberately, however, the term "flesh" (in Greek *sarx*) is used. This designates the whole human person, seen as a frail, mortal being. It does not exclude the human soul or mind. According to the biblical view of human existence we do not separately have a body or a soul/mind. We form a psychosomatic unity. We are an incarnate soul or—which refers to the same reality, only from another perspective—we are an animated body. The Logos becomes *sarx*—not that still ideal projection of the human being which in a perfect, unspoiled way would be the image of God, as shown in Plate 32. The Logos becomes *sarx*, that frail, mortal being who is tempted to prefer darkness over light, who can be deaf to God's Word and blind to God's Wisdom.

For the Greek philosophers of Jesus' time, a more paradoxical and shocking affirmation could have hardly been made. The Jews knew that the God of Abraham, Moses and David, the God of the prophets and sages acts in human history and is deeply concerned also with the material, economic and political affairs of this world. Yet even for them the confession that the Logos becomes flesh was incomprehensible.

When the prophet of the Babylonian exile was called upon to console the Israelite deportees, he had quite a different message from that of John 1:14.

What shall I cry?

*That all humankind (*in Hebrew "basar", in Greek "sarx", thus frail, mortal beings*) is grass,*

they last no longer than a flower of the field . . .
The grass withers, the flowers fade,
*but the word of our God (*in Hebrew 'dabar'*)*
endures for evermore (Isa. 40:6–8).

The consolation for these people, living the precarious existence of political prisoners and displaced persons, was the totally other, steadfast Word of God. They sang in their psalms that "the Lord's own plans shall stand for ever, and his counsel endure for all generations" (Ps. 33:11).

Now this enduring and eternally trustworthy Word of God becomes itself a highly vulnerable and stumbling human being. A new beginning is made. The prologue expresses this with the striking contrasts between the eternal being of the Logos and his historical becoming:

Verse 1 The Logos *was* turned *towards God*, and it was *God*.

Verse 14 The Logos *became* one *among us*, becoming *flesh*.

What a daring risk, to send the light into the thick of the forces of darkness! True, the darkness had until now not been able to "comprehend", or "overpower" the light (vs 5; both translations are possible, but the hymn almost certainly means the second). Yet if the world did not know him and his own people did not accept him when the Logos was full of transcendent power and glory (vss 10–11), would they know and accept the incarnate Logos in the person of Jesus of Nazareth? This was the risk which God took when the Logos became flesh.

A miniature from the early 11th century shows the risk of the incarnation (Plate 33). It is attributed to deacon Gundbald who supervised the copiers of manuscripts for the north German diocese of Hildesheim. The bishop of this diocese, Bernward, was known as a great expert in religious art. He himself might have suggested the striking symbolism of this visual interpretation of the prologue, because the miniature was to illuminate the beginning of John's Gospel in the bishop's own gospel book.

The cosmos is divided into two. In the lower half appears on the left the ocean personified in Oceanus. Like the sea, this mythical figure both supports life and brings chaos. The second aspect is emphasized here because Oceanus rides on Leviathan "that twisting sea-serpent and monster of the deep" (Isa. 27:1; Job 41). It typifies the enemy of God's good creation. Opposite Oceanus sits Gaea, mother-earth, from whom natural life originates and grows. She sits near a tree which symbolizes fertility, but in whose branches lives the snake of Genesis 3. While in the myths of antiquity Gaea is often imagined together with her children, in the miniature from Hildesheim these children have become Adam and Eve. The one holds the snake with the left hand. The other gropes for the apple which the snake temptingly presents.

The lower half portrays thus the world and humanity in their threatened and sinful condition. Yet something happens to the cosmos. Both Oceanus and Gaea, even the monster Leviathan, look up to the star in the exact centre of the miniature. This star is like a window which ends the separation between heaven and earth.

The upper half of the miniature shows, in the midst of heavenly symbols, the Logos sitting on a throne between two seraphs. He holds with his left hand the book called VITA (= "life") and with the right hand a disk showing the lamb which is touching the book of life. The youthful figure on the throne has sometimes been interpreted as God the Father according to the vision recorded in Revelation 4, where also the lamb and the book of life appear. However, the portrayal of the young ruler enthroned in heaven with the nimbus of the cross and surrounded by the golden mandorla (an almond-shaped symbol of light and majesty) resembles much more the medieval Christ in majesty than God the Father (compare Plate 2). Moreover, this miniature is presented with the prologue of John's Gospel and not with the visions of the Book of Revelation.

An early New Testament confession expresses the mystery of faith by which Christians live as follows:

He was manifested in the flesh,
vindicated in the spirit,
seen by angels;

proclaimed among the nations,
believed in throughout the world,
glorified in high heaven (1 Tim. 3:16).

While this confession starts with the incarnation, testifying to the work of Christ on earth and to his return to heaven, the miniature of Hildesheim shows how, before his incarnation, the Logos was "glorified in high heaven", but then came down to the earth and became incarnate in the threatening and sinful world, just above the jaws of Leviathan.

The visual interpretation of what happened when the Logos became incarnate anticipates already the ministry and sacrificial death of Jesus: the crib hanging by the rays of the star has the form of an altar, and in heaven the Logos appears not only as the majestic ruler of all, but also as the lamb. Only by becoming "the lamb of God who takes away the sin of the world" (Jn 1:29) can Jesus fulfill the will of the Father. Only by giving his own life as a sacrifice on the altar of the cross can Jesus become what he claims in his "I am" sayings: the "bread of life", the "light of life", the "resurrection and the life", "the way, the truth and the life" (Jn 6:35; 8:12; 11:25; 14:6).

Beneath the miniature appears the caption "Apocalypsis", "revelation". Indeed it was through his incarnation that the Logos became the definitive revealer of God's will. He who is "nearest to the Father's heart has made him known" (Jn 1:18). He is the Revelation, the Apocalypsis.

Plate 33: *"Apocalypsis". Miniature included in the first chapter of John's Gospel in the "Precious gospel book" of bishop Bernward of Hildesheim. Probably A.D. 1015.*

We saw his glory

When Peter, John and James were together with their master on the mountain of transfiguration it happened that Jesus' "face changed and his clothes became dazzling white". Then, as the disciples awoke from their deep sleep, "they saw his glory" (Lk. 9:29–32).

As was noticed earlier, the Fourth Gospel includes no transfiguration story, though one would most expect to find it in John's vision of Christ. But the whole life and work of Jesus, from the incarnation onwards until the self-giving death on the cross, is seen by John as one great transfiguration:

The Logos became flesh . . .
and we saw his glory.

The extremely simple one-line drawing by Iris Hahs-Hoffstetter shows with its colour symbolism the incarnation as a transfiguration (Plate 34). Into the cold blue and the earthy dark brown and green of our existence, a dazzling white presence has come. It begins to reflect itself. With its warmth and light it transforms the cold and dark world.

For ages such an event had been expected by all nations, especially by the people of Israel. The prophet Isaiah saw something of this happening already at the birth or enthronement of a Davidic ruler:

The people who walked in darkness
have seen a great light:
light has dawned upon them,
dwellers in a land as dark as death.
You have increased their joy and given them gladness;
they rejoice in your presence as people rejoice at harvest
(Isa. 9:2ff).

Isaiah then went on to speak about this Davidic ruler in rather military terms, but described "the boy born for us" also as the "prince of peace".

The Davidic rulers failed to bring such light and glory. Therefore the expectation centred more on a future intervention of God in history. Thus the great prophet of the exile conforted the Israelite deportees in Babylon that in a new exodus both God and God's people would return to the promised land:

Thus shall the glory of the Lord be revealed,
and all humankind together shall see it;
for the Lord himself has spoken (Isa. 40:5).

Still later, when after the exile those who had returned to Jerusalem were discouraged about the smallness of the new temple and the insignificance of the newly built town, another prophet had this message for the disheartened city:

Arise, Jerusalem,
rise clothed in light; your light has come,
and the glory of the Lord shines over you.
For, though darkness covers the earth
and dark night the nations,
the Lord shall shine upon you
and over you shall his glory appear;
and the nations shall march towards your light
and their kings to your sunrise (Isa. 60:1–3).

Then Jerusalem was again occupied by foreign powers. Now the expectation centred more and more on the coming of a future liberator, a Messiah. The inter-testamental hymn about the priestly Messiah in the Testament of Levi (compare above p. 16) describes the coming of that saviour in these words:

His star shall arise in heaven as of a king.
Lighting up the light of knowledge as the sun the day.
And he shall be magnified in the world.
He shall shine forth as the sun on the earth,
and shall remove all darkness from under heaven,
and there shall be peace in all the earth.
The heavens shall exult in his days,
and the earth shall be glad,
and the clouds shall rejoice;
and the knowledge of the Lord shall be poured forth
upon the earth, as the water of the seas
(Test. Lev. 18:3–5).

With the incarnation of the Logos in Jesus all these expectations were taken up. However, they became visible only for those who could see and believe. And after the eye-witnesses had died, the fulfilment of these expectations in Christ is only perceptible to those who believe without seeing.

The last verses in John's Gospel—before the post-script of chapter 21 added later—are about "doubting" Thomas. He had not been present when the risen Lord appeared to the other disciples. When they told him, "We have seen the Lord", he responded, "Unless I see the mark of the nails on his hands, unless I put my finger into the place where the nails were, and my hand into his side, I will not believe it" (Jn 20:24f).

It has been suggested that in this doubting Thomas we meet a typical representative of the church for which John's Gospel was written. Towards the end of the 1st century A.D. Jewish Christians were excluded from the

Plate 34: *"We saw his glory", crayon drawing by Iris Hahs-Hoffstetter, GDR. Contemporary.*

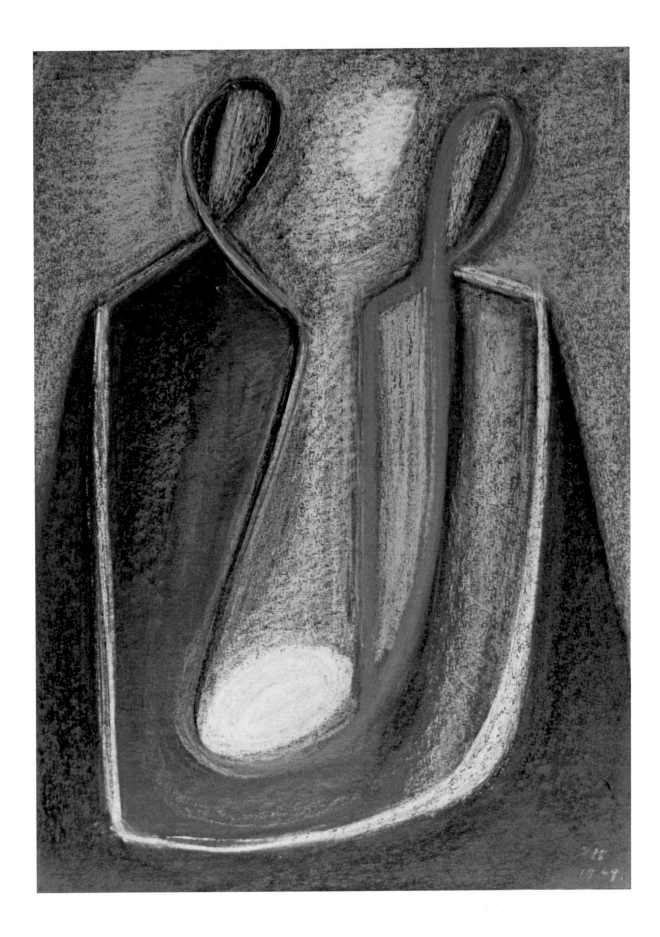

synagogues (Jn 9:22; 12:42; 16:2). Gentile Christians in Asia Minor, that melting pot of religious and popular philosophies, were confused. Moreover, sporadic persecutions of Jews and Christians began to threaten the very existence of the small and scattered Christian communities. Meanwhile most of the eye-witnesses of Jesus had died. What everybody could see at that time was that kingdom, power and glory belonged to the Roman emperor and not to Jesus, especially in the time of Domitian (A.D. 81–96).

Christians in Asia Minor were therefore in a deep crisis of faith. What in their worship assemblies they so triumphantly affirmed, was it really true? Had God really become fully human in Jesus? Could God's glory and power be seen in his work, death and resurrection? Was it worthwhile suffering for this Jesus whom they could no more see? Based on the testimony of the eye-witnesses, especially that of the beloved disciple, the writer of John's Gospel answers such questions with an emphatic "yes!"

The Logos has indeed become flesh,
He did pitch his tent among us,
We truly saw his glory!

The doubting Thomas was given the opportunity to see and touch the risen Jesus. He made his confession "My Lord and my God!" but he was also told, "Happy are they who never saw me and yet have found faith" (Jn 20:26ff).

What is this faith which John the baptist was sent to evoke (Jn 1:7) and to which the whole of John's Gospel testifies? An often overlooked line in the prologue gives us important clues: "He (the incarnate Logos) pitched his tent/tabernacle among us" (vs 14b). The sentence calls forth many echoes from the Old Testament, from inter-testamental writings and Johannine testimonies in the New Testament.

The Greek verb *skēnoun* literally means "to pitch a tent" or "to dwell in a tent". This first of all recalls the exodus story where God told Moses: "Make me a sanctuary, and I will dwell among them"—the Israelites on their journey from Sinai to Canaan (Ex. 25:8f; 40:34ff). This sanctuary had the form of a tent (*skēnē*): "Moses used to take a tent and pitch it at a distance outside the camp. He called it the Tent of the Presence . . . Whenever Moses went out to the tent, all the people would rise and stand, each at the entrance to his tent, and follow Moses with their eyes until he entered the tent. When Moses entered it, the pillar of cloud came down, and stayed at the entrance to the tent while the Lord spoke with Moses. As soon as the people

saw the pillar of the cloud . . . they would all prostrate themselves" (Ex. 33:7ff).

This "pillar of cloud", sometimes "pillar of fire", is later associated with the temple in Jerusalem (1 Kings 8:10f; Ez. 10:4f). It points both to God's hidden presence and to the manifestation of this presence in glory (theophany). The prologue affirms that the incarnate Logos, Jesus, has now become this tent where God's glory can be seen. His body is the temple (Jn 2:21). He thus anticipates the heavenly Jerusalem, where "God has pitched his tent among his people" and where the seer "saw no temple in the city; for its temple was the sovereign Lord God and the Lamb. And the city had no need of sun or moon to shine upon it; for the glory of God gave it light, and its lamp was the Lamb" (Rev. 21:3, 22f).

Another strong and certainly intentional reminiscence called forth by the verb *skēnoun* is the hymn in praise of Wisdom found in the inter-testamental book of Sirach (ca. 180 B.C.). Wisdom testifies about herself:

I am the word which was spoken by the Most High;
it was I who covered the earth like a mist.
My dwelling-place (skēnoun) was in high heaven;
my throne was in a pillar of cloud.
Alone I made a circuit of the sky
and traversed the depth of the abyss.
The waves of the sea, the whole earth,
every people and nation were under my sway.
Among them all I looked for a home:
in whose territory was I to settle?
Then the Creator of the universe laid a command upon me;
my Creator decreed where I should dwell (skēnē).
He said, "Make your home (skēnoun) in Jacob;
find your heritage in Israel . . ."
In the sacred tent (skēnē) I ministered in his presence,
and so I came to be established in Zion (Sir. 24:3–10).

This hymn of the Wisdom could well have served as a model for the hymn of the Logos in John's prologue, but there is a marked difference which the evangelist emphasizes in the closing annotation to the prologue. Sirach sees ultimately the Wisdom incarnate in the Torah, God's will and promise fixed in the Jewish Scriptures. "All this", he comments at the end of the hymn, "is the covenant-book of God Most High, the law which Moses enacted to be the heritage of the assemblies of Jacob" (Sir. 24:23). In John's prologue we see a parallel development. The Logos, who has so many similarities with the Wisdom, becomes incarnate not in a book but in a person, Jesus of Nazareth. "While the Law was a gift through Moses, grace and truth came through Jesus Christ" (Jn 1:17).

The only Son

Philo, the great Jewish philosopher of Alexandria and a contemporary of Jesus, once described the ultimate religious experience of Moses: "He grasped that God cannot be grasped by anyone, and he saw that God can precisely not be seen." Indeed when Moses asked to be shown the glory of God on Mount Sinai, he was allowed to see only the back of God whose glory passed by. He was told: "My face you cannot see, for no mortal man may see me and live" (Ex. 33:18–23; Isa. 6:5).

The inter-testamental book of Sirach rightly asks: "Has anyone ever seen God, to be able to describe him?" (Sir. 43:31). John's prologue is like an answer to that question. After testifying to the incarnation of the Logos the hymn affirms:

We have seen his glory,
the glory of an only Son coming from the Father,
filled with grace and truth.

And the evangelist concludes the prologue: "No one has ever seen God; it is God, the only Son, who is nearest to the Father's heart, who has made him known" (Jn 1:14, 18).

In both the question of Sirach and in John's affirmation about God's Son various forms of the Greek verb *exegeomai* are used which in the Bible has always the significance of "telling", "revealing", "making known" and "interpreting". Who can see and interpret God? Nobody, says Sirach. Only the Son, says the evangelist John.

For both Jews and Greeks it was nothing new to call specially endowed human persons "sons and daughters of God" or "divine men", be they royalty or miracle workers. John's prologue also talks of "children of God" (Jn 1:12). There the general Greek term for children (*tekna*) is used. The special designation *ho huios (tou theou)* = "the Son (of God)" or *monogenēs huios* = "the only Son" in John's Gospel is strictly reserved for Jesus.

Such an absolute use of the title was bound to lead to a head-on collision with the Jewish authorities. According to Mark's Good News Jesus never used this title for himself (compare above pp. 13ff). In John's testimony, however, *the* Son (of God) is a term frequently used by Jesus. When he was accused of performing a healing on the Sabbath Jesus said: "In truth, in very truth I tell you, the Son can do nothing by himself; he does only what he sees the Father doing; what the Father does, the Son does. For the Father loves the Son and shows him all his works . . . The Father does not judge anyone, but has given full jurisdiction to the Son; it is his will that all should pay the same honour to the Son as to the Father. To deny honour to the Son is to deny it to the Father who sent him . . . In truth, in very truth I tell you, a time is coming, indeed it is already here, when the dead shall hear the voice of the Son of God, and all who hear shall come to life. For as the Father has life-giving power in himself, so has the Son, by the Father's gift" (Jn 5:19–26).

It was this testimony which brought Jesus to the cross. The chief priests' main argument in their accusation before Pilate was: "We have a law; and by that law he ought to die, because he has claimed to be Son of God" (Jn 19:7). Behind this accusation there was an even greater scandal caused by the Jesus of John's Gospel.

At the beginning of the prologue the Logos is said to be turned towards God and to be God. In inter-testamental Jewish writings such an affirmation could be made of God's Word or God's Wisdom without being accused of sacrilege. Yet the prologue ends by saying about the *incarnate* Logos: "It is God the only Son, ever at the Father's side, who has revealed Him, who is the exegete" (Jn 1:18). Although the most ancient Greek manuscripts of John's Gospel transmit the text in this way, many translations leave out the designation "God" in this sentence. However, this is exactly what Jesus' opponents held against him, when they took up stones to kill him: "We are not going to stone you for any good deed, but for your blasphemy. You, a mere man, claim to be a god!" (Jn 10:33).

With this they clearly saw and expressed the scandal of the incarnation. In the fully human Jesus of Nazareth God himself was present among us. Jesus was in the most literal sense of that word the Immanuel (though that term is found only in Matthew's Gospel). By his works and words, his death and resurrection, by his very being, he became the exegete, the revealer. "Anyone who has seen me has seen the Father" (Jn 14:9).

"The Logos became flesh." No human intermediaries appear in John's account of the incarnation. Twice the baptist is mentioned in the prologue, but he was sent exclusively to bear witness to Jesus. He says he is not the messianic forerunner Elijah (Jn 1:19ff, compare above pp. 19ff), and the fourth evangelist never explicitly reports Jesus' baptism by John the baptist.

Some scholars and Bible translators see in John 1:13 a hidden reference to the extraordinary conception of Jesus and therefore also to Mary. According to some old Latin translations of John's Gospel, and following the quotations in the writings of several church fathers, they translate: "he who was begotten (singular) not by blood . . ., but by God". All Greek manuscripts, however, state unequivocally: "those who were begotten (plural) not by blood . . .". Neither the extraordinary conception nor the human intermediary Mary is mentioned in John's prologue.

Why then choose for meditation on the only Son an art work where Jesus stands on the knees of Mary, as in the sculpture from Zimbabwe reproduced in Plate 35? First of all because this African Jesus is clearly portrayed in the way in which John the evangelist saw him: He stands upright, with great dignity, and "holding the whole world in his hand", as it is sung in a Black American spiritual. One can well imagine him making the famous "I am" statements, where the Jesus of John's Gospel applies to himself the divine name "I AM" which God revealed to Moses from the burning bush (Ex. 3:1ff, 13ff).

These great sayings are the burden of a modern Indian hymn:

Jesus the Lord said: "I am the Bread
the Bread of Life for mankind am I".
Jesus the Lord said: "I am the Door,
the Way and the Door for the poor am I".
Jesus the Lord said: "I am the Light,
the one true Light of the world am I".
Jesus the Lord said: "I am the Shepherd,
the one Good Shepherd of the sheep am I".
Jesus the Lord said: "I am the Life,
the Resurrection and the Life am I".

What about Mary, on whose knees this very Johannine Jesus stands? While she is not mentioned in the prologue, the mother of Jesus plays an important role in John's Gospel. She was with her son when he transformed water into wine at the marriage feast in Cana, and she went with him to Capernaum (Jn 2:1ff, 12). People knew that she and her husband Joseph were the parents of Jesus (Jn 6:42). Above all, Mary stood, with the beloved disciple, near the cross. Before his death Jesus said to her: "Mother, there is your son"; and to the disciple: "There is your mother" (Jn 19:26f). The deeper meaning of this scene is often interpreted as a mutual adoption: on the one hand, Mary and the other women near the cross represent the believing church which needs for its life and unity the testimony of the true witness; on the other hand the disciple is as it were the personification of the good news which needs the church as its agent in the world. Others see in Mary and the disciple the Jewish and the gentile church whom Jesus commits to each other's care.

Just as John the Zebedee and the beloved disciple are never mentioned by name in John's Gospel, so also the mother of Jesus is never called by her name in that Gospel. She becomes a symbol, beyond being a historical person. Symbols are open to various interpretations. The artist certainly wanted to portray Mary as the throne of Jesus, which became a common motif in Christian art. But could we not also interpret the womanly figure of the African sculpture as the personified Wisdom of God? Earlier we saw how strongly John's prologue is influenced by the Old Testament and inter-testamental Wisdom literature (compare above pp. 101, 112). Both the Hebrew and Greek terms for wisdom are of feminine gender. When the manifestation of God as Wisdom becomes the personified Wisdom, she is always described as a woman. Accordingly the God revealed in John's Gospel is portrayed with attitudes and sentiments which often are rightly or wrongly attributed in a special way to women: he is a loving, self-giving God, working from within, letting the seed grow and the plants mature until the fruits are ripe.

Jesus, the incarnation of this God, is in the prologue described as one "filled with grace and truth" (Jn 1:14, 17). This expression almost certainly transcribes the Hebrew words *hesed* and *'emet*, which are often used in the Old Testament to describe the enduring covenant love of God. On Mount Sinai this God described himself to Moses: "The Lord, a god compassionate and gracious, long-suffering, ever constant (*hesed*) and true (*'emet*)" (Ex. 34:6). With such true and constant love the Jesus of John's Gospel seeks and maintains union with his Father and with his own (Jn 17:11–23). He waits for his hour and manifests a deep sensibility in his relations with the women he meets (Jn 4). It is little wonder that only in John's Gospel Jesus tells the parable of the woman in labour. Her waiting for her hour, and subsequently her rejoicing at the birth of the child (Jn 16:21f) are like the sorrow and joy which the disciples will experience when their Lord will die on the cross, and later rise from the dead.

Plate 35: *"The world in his hands", wood sculpture in the Catholic Church at Serima, Zimbabwe. Contemporary.*

Life for the world

A piece of wood in the form of the cross, some flowers, and the dark circle of the world. A branch of thorns which passes right through the cross with the flowers and goes beyond the border of the world to form an open circle above the cross. How does this flower arrangement of Kyoko Grant (Plate 36) relate to John's vision of the incarnation?

The prologue never explicitly mentions the passion of Jesus. True, the Logos comes as life and light into the world, and neither the world nor his own people receive him (Jn 1:10f). His light shines in the darkness, and the darkness could not overpower it (Jn 1:5). Only indirectly is the coming struggle between belief and unbelief, between life and death, light and darkness hinted at.

Nor does the prologue explicitly refer to the resurrection and the return of the incarnate Logos to God. Nevertheless, the fact that the darkness could not overpower the light points to the light's victory. Moreover, some see an evocation of Jesus' resurrection and ascension in the last sentence of the prologue which affirms that the only Son "is (present participle) ever at the Father's side" (Jn 1:18; the original Greek states: "The only Son is towards the bosom of the Father"). If this understanding is right, the whole journey of the Logos, his descent and ascent, is described in the prologue. The last verse then is seen to echo and reinforce the first verse where we see the Logos intimately turned towards God. This unity of the Father and the Son, this same perfect harmonization of their will and work, are emphasized throughout John's Gospel. The pre-existent Logos and the risen Lord are in intimate communion with God; so is the Logos incarnate.

What the prologue clearly does affirm is that through the Logos life and light have come into the world (vss 4f, 9). Through him we can become God's children (vs 12). Out of his fullness we all receive "grace in return for grace" (vs 16). Over and above the law given by the mediation of Moses, in Jesus "grace and truth"—or truly constant covenant love of God—has become manifest (vs 17).

These are great affirmations of faith. But how are they realized?

By meditating on Kyoko Grant's flower arrangement in the light of the following sayings of the Johannine

Jesus, we may be enabled to perceive something of God's work for the life of the world:

God loved the world so much that he gave his only Son, that everyone who has faith in him may not die but have eternal life. It was not to judge the world that God sent his Son into the world, but that through him the world might be saved (Jn 3:16f).

—In truth, in very truth I tell you, a grain of wheat remains a solitary grain unless it falls into the ground and dies; but if it dies, it bears a rich harvest (Jn 12:24).

—And I shall draw all to myself, when I am lifted up from this earth. This he said to indicate the kind of death he was to die (Jn 12:32).

—There is no greater love than this, that someone should lay down his life for his friends (Jn 15:13).

—It (namely the Father's will) is accomplished! (Jn 19:30).

The purpose of John's Gospel is clearly stated in its original closing sentence. What is written in this book has "been recorded in order that you may hold the faith that Jesus is the Christ, the Son of God, and that through this faith you may possess life by his name" (Jn 20:31). The incarnation and the whole ministry, death and resurrection of Jesus must instill in us that faith which leads to true life.

When the evangelist John speaks about our physical life on earth which inevitably will end in death, he uses the Greek term *psyche*. In contrast to such an ephemeral existence there is another life, a true and eternal one, which John always designates with the Greek term *zōē*. From the prologue onwards the evangelist testifies to this qualitatively different type of life. *Zōē* does not mean life after death. It begins here and now and it includes all the sufferings and joys, the illnesses and healings of life here on earth. Yet the enduring quality of that life is such that Jesus could say: "I am the resurrection and the life. The one who has faith in me, even though he die, he shall come to life; and no one who is alive and has faith shall ever die" (Jn 11:25f).

Jesus' teaching about the bread of life sheds light on this paradoxical statement as well as on some of the bold affirmations of the prologue. The context of that instruction was the Jewish Passover and the feeding of the five thousand (Jn 6:1–15). Those who then listened to Jesus were deeply shocked: "This is a hard saying: who can listen to it?" they said, and "from that time on, many of his disciples withdrew" (Jn 6:60, 66). We are here faced with the scandal of both the incarnation and the cross.

Plate 36: *Flower arrangement, by Kyoko Grant, Japan. Contemporary.*

The teaching on the bread of life (Jn 6:26–58) subsequently makes two main emphases: the first on Jesus as the Revealer who challenges us to believe; the second on Jesus as the Redeemer who invites us to sacramental communion. No clear-cut division can be made because the two themes flow into each other.

After the introductory conversation about the manna and the bread of life (vss 26–34) the first theme predominates in verses 35–50. Life is gained by coming to Jesus and believing in him who has come down from heaven to reveal the will and work of his Father. Like the first part of the prologue, so also this first part of the teaching on the bread of life is strongly influenced by the Wisdom literature. In the Proverbs the personified Wisdom invites us: "Come, dine with me and taste the wine that I have spiced" (Prov. 9:5). About the one who accepts this invitation the inter-testamental book of Sirach says: "For food Wisdom will give him the bread of understanding and for drink the water of knowledge" (Sir. 15:3). Yet those who begin to taste such food "will be hungry for more and thirst for more" (Sir. 24:21). Jesus, the incarnate Logos, responds to this longing: "I am the bread of life. Whoever comes to me shall never be hungry, and whoever believes in me shall never be thirsty" (Jn 6:35).

The knowledge of God which we receive through Jesus does not stand in opposition to the knowledge which since the beginning could be gained by God's Word and Wisdom. Yet those who are "drawn by the Father" and "taught by God" (Jn 6:44f) see now in Jesus the fuller revelation, the very source of life.

A similar progression from a partial to a fuller perception of true life is already expressed in John's prologue. Only when the Logos turned towards creation was there the possibility of true life on earth (already in Jn 1:4 the term $zōē$ is used). Men, women and children now had the possibility to see light and thus to become God's children. Like the manna in the desert, the law given through Moses was also a gift of grace. Yet when the Logos became incarnate in Jesus and pitched his tent among us, then only it became possible to know and see the glory and the true, enduring covenant love of God. (This may be the meaning of the difficult expression "grace in place of grace" in Jn 1:16.) Thus Jesus became the true exegete, the true Revealer.

What we receive out of Jesus' fullness is not only the knowledge of God's love. This love gives us the true life. Jesus the Revealer becomes also the Redeemer. This second emphasis in the teaching about the bread of life is expressed in a shockingly material way in John 6:51–58. The incarnation will lead to the passion. He who came as the Lamb of God will be slaughtered. The eye-witness of John's Gospel saw "a flow of blood and water" streaming out of the side of Jesus on the cross (Jn 19:34f). This gift of life by God's Son for the whole world has superseded the Jewish Passover.

From the early church onwards Christians recall this saving event and feel its presence in the celebration of the holy communion, the eucharist. That was what Jesus meant when he said (Jn 6:51):

I am that living bread
which has come down from heaven;
if anyone eats this bread he shall live for ever.
Moreover, the bread which I will give is my own flesh;
I give it for the life of the world.

Acknowledgments

A text like the present one, written and rewritten through a period of several years, has drawn on far too many sources, and it is not easy to recall all of them. Conversations with friends, with biblical scholars and artists during travels in five continents, and many hours of reading and reflection have gradually shaped this book. What is true of the text applies also to the long process of collecting, eliminating and choosing the art work finally included.

I want to express very special thanks to the following: Dr Margret Koch, the librarian of the Ecumenical Institute at Bossey near Geneva, who has sympathetically and critically accompanied the gradual growth of this book, its various drafts and the selection of the art. With her knowledge of the European Middle Ages, and of Roman Catholic and Orthodox spirituality, she contributed a great deal to this book—and somewhat curbed my Protestant bias. Mrs Brigitte Constant, my colleague in the Biblical Studies office of the World Council of Churches, not only faithfully typed and retyped the manuscript, but also did most of the work for getting the ektachromes of art work and in procuring the necessary permissions for quoting and reproducing. In a period when the WCC's Publications Office was overburdened by the preparations for the WCC Assembly in Vancouver 1983 and later its follow-up work, colleagues in that office spent long hours on the manuscript and in consultation with other publishers. Last but not least, I want to thank Ineke, my wife, who once again had for long periods an absent-minded husband, absorbed in reading, exegesis, photography and writing when there must have been so many other urgent tasks in home and family.

In the **biblical reflections** here no totally new exegetical insights are proposed. My aim was rather to present various possible interpretations and to indicate some of the broad convergences reached in scholarly exegesis. I consulted the major recent gospel commentaries in several languages. I also read, sifted and assimilated part of the often contradictory special exegetical studies on the prologues of Mark and John and the infancy narratives of Matthew and Luke. I do not know of any extensive study comparing the beginnings of the four gospels, except the short article by Oscar J. F. Seitz, "Gospel Prologues: a Common Pattern?", in *Journal of Biblical Literature*, 83, 1964, pp. 262–268.

I am deeply indebted to the comprehensive exegetical work by Raymond E. Brown, *The Birth of the Messiah: a Commentary on the Infancy Narratives of Matthew and Luke*, Garden City, NY, 1977. While I do not always follow the conclusions of Brown's detailed analyses of the texts, this was the study which triggered off the biblical reflections and informed them most. In Brown's book are extensive bibliographies from many language areas on Matthew 1–2 and Luke 1–2.

There are fewer specialized studies on Mark's prologue, and many concentrate only on the prophetic quotations in Mark 1:1–3 or on John the baptist and Jesus' baptism (vss 4–11) or on Jesus' temptation (vss 12–13). Several studies include also the summary of Jesus' proclamation (vss 14–15) in Mark's prologue. I followed mainly Eduard Schweizer's commentary, *The Good News According to Mark*, Richmond, VA, 1970. For an extensive bibliography see Rudolf Pesch, *Das Markusevangelium*, Vol. I, Freiburg *et al.*, 1976.

Among the many specialized studies on John's prologue I gained most insights from André Feuillet, *Le prologue du quatrième évangile*, Paris, 1968, where a comprehensive bibliography can also be found.

The primary source for the biblical reflections was obviously the Greek text of the introductory passages in the four gospels, memorized, studied and "ruminated" over a long period of time.

Concerning the **relationship between Christian spirituality and artistic interpretations** of the Incarnation I found the following studies most helpful: Michael Baily, "The Crib and Exegesis of Luke 2:1–20", in *The Irish Ecclesiastical Review*, December 1963, pp. 358–376. Henrik Cornell, *The Iconography of the Nativity of Christ*, Uppsala, 1924. Oscar Cullmann, *Der Ursprung des Weihnachtsfestes*, Zürich/Stuttgart, 1960[2]. Georges Drobot, *Icône de la Nativité*, Spiritualité orientale, no 15, Abbaye de Bellefontaine, 1975. Edgar Hennecke & Wilhelm Schneemelcher (eds), *New Testament Apocrypha*, Vol. I, London, 1963: "Infancy Gospels", O. Cullmann & A. J. B. Higgins, pp. 363–417. Paulus Hinz, *Deus Homo: Das Christusbild von seinen Ursprüngen bis zur Gegenwart*, Vol. I. and II, Berlin, 1973/1981. Adey Horton, *The Child Jesus* (a study on the influence of the apocryphal infancy gospels on medieval art), New York, 1975. Walter Lipphardt a.o., "Liturgische Dramen", in *Die Musik in Geschichte und Gegenwart*, Vol. VIII, pp. 1010–1047. Gertrud Schiller, *Ikonographie der christlichen Kunst*, Vol. I, 3rd ed., Gütersloh, 1981. Relevant entries in *Die Religion in Geschichte und Gegenwart*, Vol. I–VI, 3rd ed., Tübingen, 1957–1962.

For the **iconography of the Incarnation** see the above mentioned publications by Cornell, Drobot, Hinz and Schiller as well as the relevant articles in Engelbert Kirschbaum (ed), *Lexikon der christlichen Ikonographie*, Rome et al., 1968–1972. Günther Ristow, *Die Geburt Christi in der frühchristlichen und byzantinisch-ostkirchlichen Kunst*, Recklinghausen, 1963. For the *modern and contemporary period* no special publication on the iconography of the incarnation seems to exist. During that period artistic interpretations of the passion of Jesus far outnumber those of his incarnation. In some Christmas books examples of modern art are included, e.g. in Linda Ching Sledge, *Shivering Babe, Victorious Lord: the Nativity in Poetry and Art*, Grand Rapids, MI, 1981. For the Christian art in Asia, Africa and Latin America see the relevant texts and plates of the publications listed in my *On a Friday Noon: Meditations Under the Cross*, Geneva, 1979, pp. 87f. No studies exclusively devoted to non-Western artistic interpretations of the incarnation are known to me. Except the bibliography in the above mentioned book see Frederick Buechner & Lee Boltin, *The Faces of Jesus*, New York, 1974; Gertrud Weinhold & Harry C. Suchland, *Freude der Völker: Weihnachtskrippen und Zeichen der Christusgeburt aus aller Welt*, Munich, 1978; relevant texts and plates in the periodical *Image: Christ and Art in Asia*, Singapore/Kyoto, since 1979.

Origin of quotations

Most quotations from the Bible and from Apocrypha/ Deutero-Canonical books follow the *New English Bible* (copyright 1970 by permission of Oxford and Cambridge University Presses). However, the "Thou" and "Thine" are rendered with "You" and "Yours", and wherever the original text allows it, a more inclusive language than that of the NEB is used. Where the biblical reflection calls for it, the author has made a literal translation from the Hebrew and Greek originals. For John's prologue a slightly altered version of the translation by Raymond E. Brown was used (compare his commentary on *The Gospel According to John*, Vol. I, Doubleday & Company, Inc., Garden City, NY, 1966).

Many texts quoted in this book are free translations made by the author from the original languages or modern versions of antiquated English translations. In the following enumeration they are indicated by the reference to where the original can be found and by an asterisk. For all quotations from original English texts or existing modern English translations permission has been granted to quote.

Page 2: Jerome, "Commentary on Matthew", in Migne, *P.L.* (= Patrologiae cursus completus, series Latina), 26, 19. Compare *P.L.* 25.21f★, and "Sources chrétiennes", 242. Cerf, Paris, 1977, pp. 63–65.

Page 4: *Cantate Domino: an ecumenical hymn book*, Bärenreiter-Verlag, Kassel, 1974, No. 152 (translation G. Moultrie). For a more literal translation cf. A. Roberts and J. Donaldson (eds), *The Ante-Nicene Fathers*, Vol. VII, W. B. Eerdmans Publishing Co., Grand Rapids, MI, p. 540.

Page 7: Statements of Papias and Eusebius in Eusebius, "Church History" III.39.15 and II.15.1, in *The Nicene and Post-Nicene Fathers*, Series Two, Vol. 1, W. B. Eerdmans Publishing Co., Grand Rapids, MI, 1952, pp. 172f and 116★.

Page 10: *Tagzeitenbuch des monastischen Breviers*, Pustet, Regensburg, 1960⁴, p. 1659f★.

Page 14: *Cantate Domino*, No. 53, translation J. M. Neale.

Page 16: Tosephta Sota 13:2, in H. L. Strack-P. Billerbeck, *Kommentar zum Neuen Testament aus Talmud und Midrash*, C. H. Beck'sche Verlagsbuchhandlung, Munich, 1961³, Bd. I, pp. 125ff★. Testamentum Levi 18:2, 6ff, in R. H. Charles (ed), *The Apocrypha and Pseudepigrapha of the Old Testament in English*, Clarendon Press, Oxford, 1913, Vol. II, pp. 314ff.

Page 19: *Letter* by S. Raj, 23 September 1981.

Page 22: N. N. Glatzer (ed), *The Passover Haggadah*, Schocken Books/Ferrar, Strauss & Young, New York, 1953; and *The Passover, the Last Supper and the Eucharist*, Study Centre for Christian Jewish Relations, London, 1975. Venezuelan Christmas Carol, translated by Alvin Schutmaat.

Page 24: Testamentum Naphtali 8:4, in Charles, *op. cit.*, Vol. II, p. 339. Poem by S. Folau in Cliff White, *Seeds of the Word: Tongan Culture and Christian Faith*, PCRC, Vila (Vanuatu), 1979, p. 1.

Page 29: "Ave maris stella", English translation by Father Ralph Wright, Ampleforth Abbey Trustees. From *The Divine Office: the Liturgy of the Hours. According to the Roman Rite*, Vol. I, Collins et al., London, 1974, pp. 560f.

Page 30: Honorius of Augustodunum, "Speculum ecclesiae", in Migne, *P.L.* 172. 904★. Bernard de Clairvaux, "De laudibus virginis matris", Homilia III, in Migne, *P.L.* 183. 73★.

Page 40: *Cantate Domino*, No. 39, text by Fred Kaan, copyright Stainer & Bell, London.

Page 41: H. C. Kee, *The Origins of Christianity: Sources and Documents*, Prentice-Hall, Inc., Englewood Cliffs, NJ, 1973, p. 76★. H. R. Percival, *The Seven Ecumenical Councils*, p. 550, in the series *The Nicene and Post-Nicene Fathers*★.

Page 42: E. Hennecke & W. Schneemelcher (eds), *New Testament Apocrypha*, Lutterworth Press, London, 1963, Vol. I, p. 410 (German original published by J. C. B. Mohr). Patriarch Germanos, quoted in Georges Drobot, *Icône de la Nativité*, Abbaye de Bellefontaine, 1975, pp. 256f★.

Page 44: "Melker Marienlied", quoted in Maurus Berve, *Die Armenbibel: Herkunft, Gestalt, Typologie*, Beuroner Kunstverlag, Beuron, 1969, pp. 43f★.

Page 46: Anthony Butkovich, *Revelationes: St Birgitta of Sweden,*. Ecumenical Foundation of America, Los Angeles, 1972, pp. 29f.

Page 47: J. van Gogh-Bonger & V. W. van Gogh (eds), *Verzamelde brieven van Vincent van Gogh*, B.V. 't Lanthuys, Amsterdam-Antwerpen, 1974, Vol. I, p. 197★.

Page 48: Willem A. Visser 't Hooft, *Rembrandt and the Gospel*, SCM Press, London, 1957, p. 49.

Page 50: Arthur J. Arberry, *The Koran Interpreted*, George Allen & Unwin Ltd., London, 1955, pp. 30f.

Page 54: *CCA Hymnal*, No. 117, text by D. T. Niles, Singapore, 1974.

Page 58f: St Anthony and Martin Luther, quoted by Fidelis Ruppert, "Meditatio-Ruminatio: zu einem Grundbegriff christlicher Meditation", in *Erbe und Auftrag*, Vol. 53, 1977, p. 85★. Soeur Pierrette, *Le sacrement de la parole: un chemin·vers la communion et la prière continuelle—la mémorisation*, unpublished manuscript, p. 22★.

Page 67: Dio Cassius, Roman History, LXIII, 1–7, in *The Loeb Classical Library*, Harvard University Press, William B. Heinemann. Ian M. Fraser, *A Feast of Lessons, Poems and Carols*, multicopied, s.a., p. 10. Ignatius, "Letter to Ephesians" XIX.3, in *The Fathers of the Church*, Vol. I, The Catholic University of America Press, Washington, DC, 1947, pp. 94f (translation G. G. Walsh).

Page 68: Orthodox Christmas Vigil Service, in *The Festal Menaion*, translated by Mother Mary and Kallistos Ware, Faber & Faber, London, 1969, p. 266.

Page 70: Tertullian, "Against Marcion", III, 13, in *The Ante-Nicene Fathers*, Vol. III, W. B. Eerdmans Publishing Co., Grand Rapids, MI, 1963, p. 332. Beda Verabilis, "Excerpta et Collectanea", in Migne, *P. L.* 94:541. Translation quoted from Raymond E. Brown, *The Birth of the Messiah: a Commentary on the Infancy Narratives in Matthew and Luke*, copyright 1977 by Raymond E. Brown, reprinted by permission of Doubleday & Company, Inc., Garden City, NY, p. 199.

Page 70: Josephus, "Jewish War", I, 205, in *The Loeb Classical Library*, Harvard University Press, William B. Heinemann Ltd. Reprints 1956–61, "Josephus" Vol. II, p. 94★.

Page 74: Hsi An Tablet, translation quoted from John Foster, *The Church of the T'ang Dynasty*, SPCK, London, 1939, pp. 136f.

Page 78: Epiphany prayer in *The Divine Office*, Vol. I, p. 307. By permission of the Hierarchies of Australia, Ireland, and England and Wales.

Page 80: "Arabic Infancy Gospel in Hennecke/Schneemelcher, *op. cit.*, Vol. I, p. 408. St Bernardine of Sienna in *The Divine Office*, Vol. II, pp. 59f.

Page 82: "Pseudo-Matthew" in Hennecke/Schneemelcher, *op. cit.*, Vol. I, pp. 410 and 412f.

Page 84: Prayer by Marie B. Assaad, Egypt, written for this book.

Page 85: Josephus, "Jewish Antiquities" II, 205, 212, 215f, in *The Loeb Classical Library*, "Josephus" Vol. IV, pp. 253ff. Harvard University Press, William B. Heinemann Ltd.

Page 86: Shusaku Endo, *A Life of Jesus*, translated by Richard A. Schuchert, Charles E. Tuttle Company, Tokyo, 1979, pp. 80f, 151.

Page 88: Albert Abble, "La vierge noire", quoted from Martin Jarrett-Kerr, *Christ and the New Nations*, SPCK, London, 1966, pp. 98f. French original in *Les prêtres noirs s'interrogent*, Editions du Cerf, Paris.

Page 90: Raúl Macín, "Twelve poems for political refugees", privately printed. Poems 1 and 3.

Page 91: *Notes* from a conversation with Philip A. Moore, Georgetown, Guyana, May 1981.

Page 92: Juan Antonio Espinosa, "Todos Los Dias . . .", translation by Alvin Schutmaat.

Page 97: Suzanne de Dietrich, *And He Is Lifted Up: Meditations on the Gospel of John*, translated by Dennis Pardee, copyright 1969, Westminster Press, pp. 12f. French original *L'heure de l'élevation: à l'écoute de saint Jean*, Delachaux & Niestlé, Neuchâtel, 1966. Ireneus, "Against heresies" III.1.1, in *The Ante-Nicene Fathers*, Vol. I, W. B. Eerdmans Publishing Co., Grand Rapids, MI, s.a. p. 414★. Papias and Eusebius in Eusebius, *op cit.*, pp. 171 and 153.

Page 102: Ephraem Syrus, quoted by O. Cullmann, *Der Ursprung des Weihnachtsfestes*, Zwingli-Verlag, Zürich/Stuttgart, 1960², pp. 20f★.

Page 104: Clemens of Alexandria, "Propeptikos", XI. 114.2–3, in *The Anti-Nicene Fathers*, Vol. II, W.B. Eerdmans Publishing Co., Grand Rapids, MI, 1967, p. 203★.

Page 110: "Testamentum Levi" 18:3–5, in Charles, *op. cit.*, Vol. II, p. 314.

Page 113: Philo, "De posteritate Caini" 13–15, quoted in Annie Jaubert, *Approches de l'Evangile de Jean*, Editions du Seuil, Paris, 1976, p. 157★.

Page 114: *Cantate Domino*, No. 156, text by Dermott Monahan, from CCA Hymnal 1974.

List of plates

Plate 1: Symbols of the four Evangelists by Karl-Heinz Lötzsch, German Democratic Republic. Contemporary. By permission of the Kunstdienst der Evangelischen Kirche, Berlin.

Plate 2: "Majestas Domini", miniature in the Bible of Vivian, Tours, early Middle Ages. Bibliothèque nationale, Paris, Latin Folio 329 verso.

Plate 3: Evangelist Mark, illumination from the gospel book of Emperor Amda Seyon I (1314–1344). By permission of Gebr. Mann Verlag, Berlin, from Otto A. Jäger, *Äthiopische Miniaturen*, 1957.

Plate 4: "Balaam pointing to the star" or "Isaiah announcing the birth of Immanuel", early Christian fresco in the Priscilla catacombs, Rome, third century. Photo Held.

Plate 5: "Tree of Jesse", miniature of a Psalterium, South Germany, first half of thirteenth century. University Library, Freiburg im Breisgau, Hs. 24.

Plate 6: John the baptist, stone statue by Rafael López del Campo, San Juan, Puerto Rico. Contemporary. Photo Sandin.

Plate 7: "The fiery wheel", batik by Solomon P. Raj, India, 1980. Photo Raj.

Plate 8: "Okoné", wood sculpture by Paul Woei, Suriname. Private collection, Netherlands. Contemporary. Photo Woei.

Plate 9: "Saint Luke painting the madonna" by Rogier van der Weyden. Alte Pinakothek, Münich, WAF 1188. Photo Blauel Bavaria, Bild-Nummer 436.

Plate 10: "Annunciation", Heidelberg manuscript of *Biblia pauperum*, University Library, Heidelberg, Cod. Pal. Germ. 148, fol. 7ᵛ. First half of fifteenth century.

Plate 11: "Annunciation" by William Congdon. By permission of Pro Civitate Christiana from William Congdon, *Nel mio disco d'oro*, Assisi 1961.

Plate 12: "Annunciation" by Paul Woelfel, Nigeria. Contemporary. By permission of Pro Civitate Christiana, Assisi.

Plate 13: "Annunciation", panel painted by Edward Meli, Papua-New Guinea, 1979. Photo Catechetical Institute, Goroko.

Plate 14: Icon of nativity, Greek, end of sixteenth century. Ikonen-Museum Recklinghausen, Inv. Nr. 475. Photo Wiemann.

Plate 15: "Nativity", Heidelberg manuscript of *Biblia pauperum*, University Library, Heidelberg, Cod. Pal. Germ. 148, fol. 9ᵛ. First half of fifteenth century.

Plate 16: "Adoration of the shepherds" by Rembrandt, 1646. By courtesy of the Trustees, The National Gallery, London.

Plate 17: "The holy family and three biblical figures" by an unknown Hindu artist. By courtesy of the Trustees of the Prince of Wales Museum of Western India, Bombay. Not to be reproduced without prior permission of the Trustees.

Plate 18: Christmas crib made with bamboo from Taiwan, contemporary. From Sammlung und Forschungsstelle "Das Evangelium in den Wohnungen der Völker". Photo Ute Franz.

Plate 19: Christmas crib sculptured by Alfred Mlangeni, South Africa. Contemporary. From Sammlung und Forschungsstelle "Das Evangelium in den Wohnungen der Völker". Photo Ute Franz.

Plate 20: Isaiah carrying Matthew on his shoulders, thirteenth century. Cathedral of Chartres, France. Photo Fiévet.

Plate 21: Clipeus sarcophagus (detail), Rome, ca. 315. Photo Alinari.

Plate 22: Two Magi/kings, painted panel on ceiling of St Martin's church in Zillis, Switzerland, first half of twelfth century. Photo Wirz. By permission of Walter-Verlag, Olten.

Plate 23: Nestorian tablet of Hsi-An (detail), erected in AD 781. Photo Oikoumene.

Plate 24: "Adoration", wood sculpture by Nacius Joseph, Haiti. Contemporary. Private collection, Haiti. Photo Weber.

Plate 25: "Flight to Egypt", illumination from the gospel book of King David (1508–1540), Ethiopia, early sixteenth century. By permission of Gebr. Mann Verlag, Berlin, from Otto A. Jäger, *Äthiopische Miniaturen*, 1957.

Plate 26: (a) "Welcome to Egypt", Byzantine miniature, eleventh century. Bibliothèque nationale, Paris, GR. 74, fol. 4vº. (b) Modern Egyptian painting by Little Sisters of Jesus, Cairo. Photo Weber.

Plate 27: "Flight to Egypt", colour print by Sadao Watanabe, Japan, 1979. Asian Christian Art Association, Kyoto.

Plate 28: "Flight to Egypt", oil painting by Francis Sekitoleko, Uganda, 1980. Private collection. Photo Oikoumene.

Plate 29: "No room", painting by Philip A. Moore, Guyana. Contemporary. Photo Moore.

Plate 30: "In principio erat verbum", title page of John's Gospel in the Book of Kells, Ireland, second half of eighth or early ninth century. University of Dublin, Trinity College. Photo Green Studio.

Plate 31: "Christ as sol invictus", early Christian mosaic, Necropolis under St Peter, third or fourth century. Photo Held.

Plate 32: "The Logos envisaging the human being", also known as "God creating the birds envisages Adam in his mind". Sculptured relief, Cathedral of Chartres, France, thirteenth century. Photo Houvet.

Plate 33: "Apocalypsis", miniature to the first chapter of John's Gospel in the "Precious gospel book" of Bishop Bernward of Hildesheim, probably AD 1015. Domkapitel Hildesheim.

Plate 34: "We saw his glory", crayon drawing by Iris Hahs-Hoffstetter, German Democratic Republic, 1969. Photo Kunstdienst der Evangelischen Kirche, Berlin.

Plate 35: "The world in his hands", wood sculpture in the Catholic church at Serima, Zimbabwe. Contemporary. By permission of Mambo Press, Gwelo, from the book *Serima*.

Plate 36: Flower arrangement by Kyoko Grant, Japan. Contemporary. Photo Grant.